Contents

FIERCE
Love

Every reader is
an author's best
friend ♡
       All the best —
       Kim Gjerde

FIERCE Love

ONE WOMAN'S REMARKABLE JOURNEY
TO ADOPT HER DAUGHTER FROM GUATEMALA

KIM GJERDE

Kim Day
Publishing

FIERCE LOVE: ONE WOMAN'S REMARKABLE JOURNEY TO
ADOPT HER DAUGHTER FROM GUATEMALA

Copyright © 2019 by Kim Gjerde

Published by Kim Day Publishing, LLC, Frederick, Maryland

Paperback ISBN: 978-0-578-57824-8

This memoir is a truthful recollection of actual events in the author's life. Some conversations have been recreated and/or supplemented. Furthermore, the names and identifying details of some individuals have been changed to respect their privacy.

Printed in the United States of America

For Lily, may you always know how fiercely you are loved.

Introduction

 he police chief barked commands into a megaphone in
a language I was familiar with but not yet proficient.
Everyone ran for their houses. Manuel, usually calm, immediately grasped my forearm and pulled me into the house. I
understood that I was in danger, though I wasn't sure why.
Then it clicked as I looked over my shoulder. Camila, tiny but
mighty, ordered two neighboring Guatemalans to grab Lily's
small hands and take her out of there. That was my baby girl,
and she was being shuttled away. Where would we meet up
again? More important, would she be safe? Panic was rising
within me.

Once inside, Manuel shoved me hard into the stark,
cramped bathroom and ordered me to hide. My scoliosis-rid-
den spine throbbed with pain. I crouched behind the small
white toilet, struggling to breathe as the smell of the urine and
feces assaulted me. I felt like I was going to vomit.

I was terrified; I needed God's help. I closed my eyes tightly and lifted silent prayers to heaven. "Please don't give the
police any reason to search this house, please," I begged. Suddenly, I heard a rifle cock as the sound of combat boots struck

the tile floor next to the closed bathroom door. I wanted to sit down and squeeze myself even smaller behind the porcelain john, but the fear of making any noise paralyzed me. I sucked in my breath, so as not to be heard. Would I be raped and beaten, left for dead, another nameless victim in the ghettoes of Guatemala? Would I be taken to jail on suspicion of child trafficking, or extorted for money? I strained my ears to catch bits and pieces of the conversation, but none of it made any sense.

Chapter 1

The alarm clock buzzed at 5 a.m. I jumped out of bed; my heart was racing. Olav and I had to be at Johns Hopkins hospital for our last IUI cycle in the next two hours. After ten previously unsuccessful infertility attempts, we had decided this would be our last one. With my body pumped full of hormones, I was emotionally exhausted from experiencing stress-induced panic attacks.

An hour later, I had the final vial of Olav's precious seed tucked tightly to my breast to keep it warm. We were driving down the interstate to the outpatient fertility center in Northern Baltimore when I heard Olav curse under his breath. I tensed up. Olav slammed on the brakes and swerved right. The brakes howled, and we stopped within centimeters of the car in front of us. My relief lasted only microseconds. Then more screeching brakes just before the car behind us slammed into our rear bumper, jerking us forcefully forward into the car in front of us. I placed my hands over my breast in a protective grip so the vial could not escape.

The domino effect continued as the cars in back of us

slammed into one another. We were now part of a multi-car pile-up.

"Oh my gosh! Oh my gosh! Our IUI appointment!" I know I should have been concerned about the safety of the drivers and passengers, but all I could think of was our very last perfectly timed fertility appointment and how it might never happen.

I frantically searched for my cell phone and called the fertility clinic. "Hello, can you hear me?" The sound of ambulances and police sirens made it hard for me to hear the person on the other end.

"Yeah, I can hear you."

The voice sounded far away, but I was able to explain that we wouldn't make it in time for our IUI appointment. "This is Kim Gjerde. I have a 9 a.m. appointment. We just got into a multivehicle accident on I-95. I know you close at ten. Can you please stay open a little longer so we can get there?"

The woman told me she would check with the doctor. I held my breath, waiting one minute, then two. She came back on the line. "Kim, I spoke with the doctor, and they will wait."

"Thanks so much." I had never felt so grateful in my life.

"Drive carefully," she replied.

Upon our arrival, they swiftly took us into the sterile medical room where my curly- haired doctor placed the warm ultrasound gel on my abdomen. All eyes were on the screen.

The doctor's voice was promising, "Kim, it appears as though you have four healthy eggs. There is a great chance of multiples."

Olav pumped his arm in victory. "Yes!" he exclaimed, happy to feel like we might actually have the upper hand.

My head spun, slightly freaked out by the thought of multiples, and yet with four eggs I felt that at least one of them would take. This cycle was sure to work.

The next two weeks felt like an eternity. Even though it was strongly discouraged, I went out and bought several pregnancy tests, taking one each day, holding it up to the bright light in the bathroom, squinting as though I could will it to turn pink. "Please, God. Let there be a double pink line. This one just has to work." I held out hope as I swore I felt implantation cramping just the other day.

Two weeks to the day, I was greeted by my familiar red friend. I ran into my bedroom and threw myself onto our king-size bed. I screamed and pounded my fists on the mattress in rage.

"Why, God? Why me? It's not fair! Everyone else can have a baby but me."

Gradually my anger morphed into deep sobs of sadness. I curled into a ball and rocked back and forth on my unmade bed. I was a failure, unable to perform the most visceral of tasks. I couldn't give my husband the second chance at fatherhood he had so desperately wanted. And even though initially I had been apprehensive about being pregnant, after two years of trying, I had come to crave the magical experience of having a human being fluttering inside my belly and giving life to a little person. Now that little human being who would have Olav's piercing blue eyes or ringlets of my soft blond hair would never be.

As my sobs gave way to exhaustion, I heard God quietly whisper, "You will adopt." Immediately an overwhelming sense of peace washed over me. I felt an enormous weight lift off my shoulders. This was exactly what I needed to hear. I had always wanted to adopt, but I'd always felt like I owed it to both my husband and myself to at least try to have one biological child.

Now the thought of adopting gave me hope and something to be excited about. Though I had heard that the adoption process could be expensive and time-consuming, it didn't feel as difficult as infertility treatments. In fact, it felt like the easy way to build our family. I knew if we stayed the course, we would be parents. It was no longer a question of *if* we would become parents but *when*. Olav and I were both emotionally and financially ready to be parents. Olav had a steady income as a computer draftsman for a local cabinet company, and I was a physical education teacher. Adoption wasn't the consolation prize; it was the natural option. We would find a child in need of a family and hopefully give him or her a life of opportunities. Plus, I would be able to pay forward all the faithful and sacrificial love I received, as I had been adopted myself—not because I was orphaned, but simply because my father had run off one day and never came back.

I still remember the day my father announced his plans. I was twelve years old living with my mother, Avis, and my stepdad, Jay, whom my mom had married two years earlier.

We lived in modest two-story townhouse thirty minutes outside of Washington, DC. My father lived with my stepmother, whom I had known since I was five. They had met at a square dancing convention and didn't live too far from us. As a child, I spent the weekdays with my mom, but every other weekend, I looked forward to my dad picking me up from daycare for the weekend. We would do fun and adventurous things like biking on the C&O canal and hiking at Great Falls National Park. That year, at our annual family Passover Seder, hosted by my Bubby (my father's mother), my father's entire side of the family gathered to celebrate, including my aunts, uncles, cousins, and little sister. We savored the homemade matzo ball soup, and the adults enjoyed the sweet Manischewitz wine. My father looked over at my stepmom and excitedly announced, "We have decided to pursue our lifelong dream. We will be sailing around the Caribbean for the next six months."

He described how they would spend some time exploring the Bahamas and then head to the crystal blue waters of the US Virgin Islands and Puerto Rico. It sounded so exciting. But the more my father talked, the more I realized how hard it would be for me. I had a difficult time saying goodbye to them every two weeks; I didn't know how I would do with six months.

They must have had the time of their lives, because six months came and went, and they didn't return. A year came and went. Then five years. Then ten. Sporadic letters or phone calls would arrive by coercion of my beloved bubby, detailing what an amazing time they were having and how they had no regrets. The limited contact did much more harm than good. My mom and my counselor told me it had nothing to do with me, but I didn't believe them. Only those who weren't good enough got left behind. He wasn't there to teach me to drive or celebrate my graduations. It would have been better for him to have died, so as not to be continuously reminded of the weight of his absence.

In my biological father's place, my stepdad Jay, who never had any children of his own, stepped up to the plate and raised me as his own flesh and blood. Jay was a former Navy seaman who served in Vietnam. He was kindhearted, but his authoritarian style of parenting was a significant contrast to the loose and sometimes chaotic style of being raised by a single working mom for so many years. Over time, my sister and I wore down his rigidness, and we probably softened a little too. He became our dad.

"Would you like me to adopt you?" he asked me one day, with my mother hovering nearby. While my little sister was unsure, I exclaimed a definite "Yes!" More than anything, I wanted to be adopted, to know that I mattered, that I was worth it. Unfortunately, a legal adoption never occurred. I just assumed it was too complicated for my mom to get my biological father to sign away his custodial rights since he wasn't even residing in the country, and while I guess she could have had them terminated legally, it was probably just another battle she didn't have the stamina to face. For me, it was okay. I was Jay's; I didn't need a piece of paper to tell me that.

Chapter 2

At age thirty-four, even though I had always wanted to adopt, I didn't know how to begin. There was a sweet boy in a PE class I taught whose mom I knew. She and her husband had successfully adopted him as an infant from South Korea. I called her up, and she referred me to Catholic Charities, a large philanthropic organization which had a family services division that specialized in placing children both domestically and internationally into loving and safe homes.

A week later, in October 2005, we attended an informational session at the Catholic Charities office in downtown Baltimore. In the large auditorium, a panel of adoptive parents with their adopted children sat onstage. One couple named Mark and Jody were surrounded by their two beautiful school-age children from South Korea and in Jody's lap was their third child. A recently adopted ten-month-old little boy named Min-Ho, also from South Korea. He was charming the audience with his irresistible smile. He flailed his legs and grasped for his mom's necklace. I was immediately captivated by him. I didn't even hear what anyone else was saying. I was sold. I wanted to adopt a little boy from South Korea.

We left the informational session with a large packet of information to sort through.

That evening while sitting at our kitchen table, Olav leafed through the adoption information. "I don't think I am cut out for domestic adoption," he said.

Olav had two sons from a previous marriage, and he had wanted to be a dad again for so many years already. Now the idea of waiting for an indefinite amount of time to be "picked" by someone because they judged him to be worthy seemed unbearable.

"Me neither," I admitted.

It felt like a bad popularity contest from high school; one we could never win. After all, the couples who adopted domestically appeared to be younger and wealthier, picture-perfect families in every way.

"Plus, there are no set fees," Olav explained. "We wouldn't have an idea of the cost up front." One domestic adoption could cost only ten to twelve thousand dollars, while another one could cost over fifty thousand dollars. "What do you think about Russia?" Olav asked. Some friends of ours had two adopted little ones from Russian, and Olav adored them.

"Russia?" I asked. I wasn't so sure. "We have several adopted kids from Russia at school, and they have big issues." I thought of six-year-old Aleksei, who was born with fetal alcohol syndrome. He ran around my gymnasium, screaming in distress during every gym class. The other students covered their ears, trying desperately to focus on the lesson. "Aleksei has threatened to burn down the school, and there have been reports of him trying to kill his dog. Plus, to be honest, I was thinking we would adopt a child who wasn't white." I had traveled a lot in my twenties and early thirties and loved the colorful diversity of different cultures. I wanted that rainbow represented in my life. "What about South Korea? That little boy at the informational seminar was so adorable, wasn't he? He came home pretty young, and the adoption process seemed pretty straightforward."

"Yeah, but I want to be guaranteed a girl, and with South Korea we don't get to choose." Olav wanted the experience of raising a little girl. "What do you think about Guatemala?" Olav asked, pointing out the information in the packet. In Guatemala, the kids were in foster care for a maximum of six to nine months. "It seems pretty quick. They charge a flat fee, and we can choose a girl."

I had never thought of Guatemala; I'd always thought we'd adopt from China or South Korea. "I do have a student adopted from Guatemala, but she has been a handful."

"Come on, Kimmie. One kid is not representative of an entire country."

"I know, it's just so hard to choose a country. If we had a baby, we wouldn't get to choose its gender, its ethnicity, or its age. Picking like this feels weird."

Over the next few days, I pored over images online of little Guatemalan girls. The screen filled up with darling copper-skinned girls dressed in Guatemalan *huipiles* and *cortes*—embroidered blouses and woven skirts—their thick black hair pulled back tightly in braids or pigtails. Some had a shy tight-lipped smile for the camera. Others, caught in the middle of an infectious giggle, showed off their missing teeth. These children were radiant. Their joyful spirits emanated out of them despite their circumstances. I wanted that beauty in my own life; we decided to pursue an adoption of a precious little girl from Guatemala.

Catholic Charities used Project Oz as their contact for facilitating Guatemalan adoptions, so instead of going through Catholic Charities as the intermediary, we decided to go directly with Project Oz. We called a few of their references, and all of them were glowing.

A few months after giving up on IUI treatments, we nervously sat in a conference room at Project Oz. Heidi, the director of the Guatemalan adoption program, was professionally dressed in a smart navy blue pantsuit. She pulled out a large foldable timeline. "First," she explained, "you will need a home study where we will look into your family dynamics, finances, health, and driving history. We will also visit your home, which will allow us to evaluate your eligibility to adopt a child."

I immediately tensed up. Wow! This was tough stuff. Anybody could have a baby, but now someone else would decide whether we were eligible to be parents. It just didn't seem right. I thought of all the reasons we might be rejected. What if they found out I was an anorexic in my late teens and twenties? What if they learned I was taking medication to help me manage my anxiety from infertility? What if they found out Olav had been using alcohol as a coping mechanism?

I tried to make my next question sound casual. "And if we don't pass?"

Beth, a mousy brown-haired social worker, who seemed used to pulling out her calm, soothing voice in times of crisis, did her best to reassure us. "Try to relax," she said. "A home study is standard protocol with adoptions. Unless we pull up major dirt on your family, like a criminal record or child abuse or neglect, most home studies fly through without any issues."

I let out a deep sigh of relief. "Okay, what's next?"

Heidi pointed to the flowchart. "You will need to petition and be approved by the US government to adopt a foreign child under two years of age. This will require filling out some paperwork and getting some fingerprints done."

This seemed doable. We had been to the United States Citizenship and Immigration building in Baltimore plenty of times due to my husband's immigration status. He had been born in Norway and has had to renew his green card several times, so that part of the process was not totally foreign to us.

"Once you turn in all this paperwork, we will compile what is called a dossier. This will be the information we send to Guatemala to begin the official adoption process."

"What kind of timeline are we looking at?" Olav asked.

"From the time you decide to sign a contract with us to the time we send your dossier to Guatemala is about three months," Beth said. "Currently, adoption timelines for Guatemala are running about six to nine months." I squeezed Olav's hand, if all went well, we would be parents by my thirty-fifth birthday!

Chapter 3

*H*ome study? Check.

Immigration? Check.

Dossier? Check.

By March 2006, we had completed all our prerequisites, and Project Oz sent us the adoption agreement. We read through the adoption agreement; it seemed very straightforward.

"What about this clause?" Olav asked, showing me the paper. "It says the adoptive parents agree not to engage in any third-party interference. Failure to comply will be grounds to terminate the adoptive parents' adoption application."

"Why on earth would we need to engage a third party?" I wondered out loud.

"Who knows," Olav said. "It should be fine; let's just sign it."

We sent in our initial payment of twenty thousand dollars for in-country legal fees with our signed application. Prior to pursuing adoption, we wondered, how on earth would we ever be able to afford this? Friends and family came to our rescue without us even asking. Between a home equity loan and their generous gifts of seven thousand dollars, we figured we would manage.

Three weeks later, Olav was playing his acoustic guitar in the living room. He was practicing a song he had recently written and wanted to debut for his friends at his fortieth birthday party later that evening.

"Come quickly!" I screamed to Olav from the study into the living room.

Olav rushed into the room, guitar still strapped to his chest, "What's the matter?" he asked.

"Look, honey, a referral e-mail from Project Oz." The subject line read: Referral: Lilian Rosmery Cajas Ramírez.

Olav knelt beside me. With trembling hands, I clicked on the e-mail and began to read. "Lilian Rosmery Cajas Ramírez. Born April 3, 2006, in Mixco, Guatemala. 5 lbs. 6 oz."

Attached were several photographs and a pediatric health report. I clicked on the jpg attachments. A tiny baby girl lying on a pink fleece "Hello Kitty" blanket with her delicate eyelids closed.

"Look at her. Our baby girl. I can't believe it!" I screamed. I thought for sure we'd have to wait much longer for a referral.

Olav was speechless, but I could see him instantly being taken in by the photographs.

"Oh my gosh, look at her! What an amazing birthday gift!" I said.

Finally, Olav found his voice and, as always, cracked a joke to soften the intensity of the moment. "She is dressed like she is ready for a Norwegian snowstorm," he said. She was bundled from her neck to her toes in an oversized pink and white knitted sweater and sweater pants.

As we pored over the images before us, we were captivated by the gentle round shape of her little cherub face and perfectly pouted little red lips. There was a tiny red fingernail scratch on her left cheek. Her face was covered in dark lanugo. Her perfectly shaped round head was covered with small wisps of black hair. "Look how hairy she is," we said simultaneously with a laugh.

We were parents. We were in love. She was our daughter. These images represented our hope, our future, and our forever family.

Chapter 4

How's the DNA submission coming along?" I asked Karen two weeks later.

For the past four months, since November, Heidi had been our point of contact, but she had mysteriously resigned. DNA submission was the first hurdle we had to cross. It was a procedural safeguard to make sure that the child placed for adoption was actually related to the person claiming to be the mother.

"Sorry, Kim. It was rejected this week. The US Embassy said the photographs were too light; we'll resubmit shortly." I could tell from the sound of her voice she was diligently working on it. We'd hear from her shortly. I just had to be patient.

A few days passed. Still no word. I was eager to know if Lily's DNA and her birth mother's DNA had been a match, so I called Karen again.

"Yes, the results were submitted and rejected again, but I'll call Camila, my adoption facilitator, tomorrow. We'll see if we can get it resubmitted this week."

I wasn't sure why the results would be rejected but figured this was just the way the process worked. "Who's Camila? I thought we were working with Javier?"

It almost sounded as if she were covering her tracks or something. "Oh, yes, of course. Javier is your lawyer. Camila works with him." That made sense, so I didn't think anything else of it.

This back and forth continued for several more weeks. Finally, after the fourth rejection, I started to get frustrated. I told Karen we had planned to go on our visit trip to meet Lily prior to the end of the summer before I had to return to work. "Do you think we should still plan on going?"

"Definitely. The issue should be resolved quickly, and if not, you can go to the US Embassy and raise a stink."

Even though visiting Lily without confirmation of her adoptability was a risky decision, we had confidence that Karen knew what she was talking about.

Chapter 5

How strange it was to be planning a trip to visit our future daughter as my mother was dying of cancer. I was going to become a mom, and I needed my mom. However, the breast cancer that she had beaten once before had returned.

Over the next two weeks, I lovingly cared for my mother. My dad and I set up a rented hospital bed, in her formal sitting room of her lakefront home facing the beautiful vista of the water. She adored that view, the way the mist rose off the lake in the early morning and the way the blue heron glided low, almost touching the water with its wings. I spent most of my time spoon-feeding my mother tiny bits of food and giving her small amounts of water through a syringe. I was amazed by how she could subsist on so little. Her once statuesque frame had become very thin and frail. One day I asked her, "Mom, why do you continue to hold on?"

In typical Avis fashion, she replied, "For the challenge." She wasn't going to go down without a fight. Why would I expect anything different from my mom? That evening, I tenderly bathed her with a sponge and then rubbed warm lotion on her arms and legs. I could feel the bony tumors growing and spreading underneath her skin. During her last days before she could no longer speak, she gazed up at me with her big brown eyes and said, "Kimberly, you're my very best friend. I can see the love in your eyes." I was so thankful that even without words, she knew how much I loved her.

As her days with us grew shorter, my mom began to drift in and out of consciousness. She no longer wanted to eat or drink. She began to get agitated and kept trying to get out of bed even though she was too weak to do so. My dad and I had to medicate her to keep her safe. I felt so guilty. *What kind of daughter drugs her mother?* I thought. The hospice staff reminded me this was the natural process of her body shutting down. Before we knew it, she was no longer conscious. I curled up beside her on the bed, gently singing Barry Manilow's "I Can't Smile Without You," a song her daddy, my beloved Pop-Pop, sang to me. I wanted to let her know it was okay. She could let go. Her father was waiting for her.

As I sat by her bed watching her chest rise and fall at more irregular intervals, and her breaths became further and further apart, I wondered how I would know when she left me. Would I be afraid? Or would it be strangely peaceful and beautiful?

Leave it to my mom to have a final act of protection and control even in death. She wanted to spare us the heartache of watching her leave this world, and she wanted to leave on her own terms. So on the evening of July 26, 2006, my dad and I both stepped away for a brief moment. My dad went outside for a walk in the cool summer evening to clear his head, and

I went upstairs. Moments later, I came back down just in time to see my mother take her final breath. Then she was gone.

A wise friend once said, you will never understand the fierce love of a mother until you become one. My mama loved me fiercely, and with her death, she passed on the mothering baton to me. Two weeks later, in August 2006, Olav and I were on a plane to Guatemala City to meet our beautiful little angel Lilian. She was just four months old.

Chapter 6

*O*ur agency gave us a lengthy checklist of items to bring: bottles, burp cloths, clothes, and diapers, just to name a few. I neatly folded up the precious outfits, marveling at how cute each one was before placing them in my well-loved Ricardo Beverly Hills grey suitcase. I couldn't wait to dress her up.

I had heard horror stories of difficult landings in Guatemala City due to the short airport runway and construction; however, we landed without any issues. We wandered through the airport terminal, which was under heavy construction, and followed the crowds toward the exit signs. Unlike the United States where there is ample signage and everything is well-organized, in Guatemala there are rows of galvanized metal crowd-control barriers wrapped in bright yellow caution-tape separating hordes of people anxiously waiting for their loved ones. I scanned the sea of unfamiliar faces as my heart pounded wildly in my chest. I finally saw a small man dressed in a bellhop uniform holding up a small scrap piece of paper with our last name printed on it.

When we arrived at the Marriott, one of three popular

places for adoptive families to stay, the driver buzzed us into the gated compound. The gates and the fences around the hotel compound were heavily guarded by multiple armed men dressed in bulletproof vests. Ironically, Zone 10, also called Zona Viva, was considered one of the safest zones in Guatemala. I shuddered to think what the other zones might look like.

Along the side of the road, armed men dressed in khaki and black uniforms accentuated with black combat boots and holding semi-automatic rifles stood like statues guarding the office buildings, parking lots, and stores. No wonder they warned adoptive parents not to leave the hotel with their prospective children.

Lily was supposed to arrive at 2 p.m., so Olav and I headed to the lobby. There were half a dozen couples seated on the sofas. It looked like any other Marriott, except that the sofas were filled with mostly light-skinned couples cooing over their brown-skinned infants.

A few minutes later, an interpreter who introduced himself as Miguel rushed in. "Your adoption facilitator and your baby are running late. They got caught in traffic and will be here any minute."

This was the moment we had been waiting for, and now we had to wait a little bit longer. In America, time is a religion. In Central America, however, time is relative. I glanced up at the clock over the reception desk. The tiny needle of the second hand slowly clicked off the seconds, then minutes, then an hour. I was going stir crazy. To calm my growing agitation, I began to pace the hotel lobby floor, counting the tiles between the entrance door and the sofa where we eagerly waited for Lily—twenty-five tiles, to be exact. My soft-soled sandals wore a faint pathway on the newly polished marble floors.

What seemed like hours later, Camila, the facilitator, arrived through the back entrance door. Her high heels clicked as she crossed the lobby, trailed by a couple in their thirties, who I assumed must be the foster parents, and two men, Manuel and Juan, who turned out to be her brothers. I bolted toward them, leaving Olav a few steps behind.

The foster mother reluctantly handed the massive bundle of blankets over to me. She was hovering over me as, if I had never held a baby before. I gently peeled back the layers of blankets and immediately recognized our beautiful Lily tucked inside with her chubby little face and nest of thick black hair. I wrapped her in my arms, pressing her petite little infant body close to my own. I felt the warmth of her presence and covered her sweet head and face with kisses as big wet tears streamed down my cheeks. Olav wrapped his strong arms around us both and just held us. Our lives had been barreling toward this day. Motherhood had found me at last! The loss of my mother and our long struggle with infertility had led us to this precious moment.

When it was time for us to spend time alone with Lily, tears welled up in her foster mother's eyes as she embraced Lily goodbye. She let her grasp linger as though searing herself into Lily's memory. They were like new parents leaving their child for the first time, unsure if we would love her as tenderly as they had.

We promptly took Lily up to the room and removed the four layers of clothing she was bundled up in even though it was eighty degrees outside. As far as Lily was concerned, we were strangers. We sounded different, smelled weird, and probably didn't mix her Nido brand baby formula the way she was used to, but Lily was incredibly adaptable.

The next few days were a whirlwind. We had heard horror stories of parents pacing the halls late into the evening with an inconsolable child in their arms, but Lily appeared unaffected by the transition. She loved being carried in the Babybjörn and spent many happy hours dangling as she was strapped to Olav or my chest. Even though everything was new, she was a great eater and a fantastic sleeper. She would sleep for hours at a time. We would just sit and gaze at her, eagerly waiting for her to finally wake up so we could play with her. What an incredible privilege it was to adopt her.

We spent our days hanging out by the pool; in the "adoptive family room," which housed toys and books for adoptive families to hang out; and eating at the in-house restaurants. One early afternoon we were eating lunch in the American-style bar—complete with professional baseball and football jerseys—when a group of adoptive parents gathered around a petite blond woman with what appeared to be an older child strapped to her chest. I walked over to get a better sense of the conversation and learned she was exasperated with her adoption agency, whose name was not familiar to me. "She's nearly twelve months," she said. "This has been a nightmare."

I turned to Olav. "I sure hope that won't be us."

With each passing day, I realized our time together was coming to an end. I began to sob each night at the fact, knowing I was going to have to give Lily back and leave. All those years I wasn't sure I wanted to be a mother, but now that I'd met her and knew that tomorrow she would no longer be in my arms, I was broken like a glass that had shattered on the floor. I was not going to be alright; I was her mother, and she was grafted into my soul.

On our last day, I reluctantly handed her back to her foster family who was eagerly waiting for her in the hotel lobby. I sobbed uncontrollably, collapsing into my husband's arms as they walked out with her.

Goodbye, sweet Lily. I love you.

Once we got home, I couldn't stand the separation from Lily. The first week back, I couldn't stop crying. I had a hard time going to work. Every student reminded me of the sweet baby girl I had left in Guatemala. I was ready to give up everything just to be with her. In the quiet of my room, I called out to God, seeking His guidance: "Lord, I need your discernment. I really want to go to Guatemala and foster Lily, but should I?"

One day, I heard God's confident voice say, "Go!"

I called Karen to tell her my plan: I wanted to go to Guatemala and foster Lily until the adoption came through.

But Karen was not on board. "Just trust me," she said. "Lily will be home very shortly. Please, just be patient."

"Patient! I don't want to be patient!" I screamed silently to myself. I had waited to become a mother for the past two years, and now that we had met our beautiful daughter, she was part of us. I needed to be with her.

I felt so trapped, but I didn't want to go against the "hand that fed me," so to speak. Sensing my hesitation, Karen said, "You can go and visit Lily as often as you need to, and we will work diligently to bring her home as quickly as possible."

With the support of my friends and family, I committed to visiting her every five to six weeks, figuring I would have to go one or two times more. How could I have foreseen that six trips later, she would still be nowhere close to coming home?

Chapter 7

It was October 2006, six weeks since meeting Lily, and it seemed as if the process was moving forward. Karen assured us that everything was progressing according to plan. She told us Lily's case had been submitted to the Guatemalan Family Court and had been completed. Her DNA test finally came back as 99.9% positive match, and we were simply waiting for embassy pre-approval before entering PGN. This was great news as the PGN (Procuradoría General de la Nación) was the government agency in Guatemala in charge of approving all adoption cases. It was one of the final steps in the adoption process. If everything went smoothly, Lily could be with us in the United States in just a few short weeks.

Expecting this would be my second and final visit to Guatemala before bringing Lily home, I decided to bring my beloved stepdad, Jay, with me, so that he could meet his long-awaited granddaughter. Though we were still grieving my mother's death, the idea of seeing Lily filled us with hope.

On this trip, we booked a hotel in Antigua, a picturesque Spanish colonial town about forty-five minutes north of Guatemala City. We anxiously waited outside our hotel, standing next to a decorative iron window grill overflowing with purple geraniums. Finally, a beat-up faded red Datsun pulled up alongside the front of our hotel, filling the front entrance with exhaust fumes. Camila stepped out of the car. Her light blue jeans were practically painted on, accentuating her petite but curvy figure. I don't know how she didn't trip and fall as she walked in stiletto heels across the cobblestone sidewalk with Lily in her arms. I raced toward her and reached for Lily. After covering her sweet cherub face with kisses, I gazed at her. She was just like I remembered: the same chunks of baby fat, little wisps of black hair, and the same trusting eyes.

Camila handed her over to me, and to my relief, instead of crying, Lily looked up at me and reached for my hand. As I grasped her tiny fingers, I whispered, "Hi there, baby bean," a sweet nickname we had started calling her from our last visit. "You're my baby girl. And I'm your mama. I'm going to love you and know you forever."

It was strange but she looked at me, and it was almost like she understood what I had said.

The next day, after a full night of sleep in her Pack 'n Play crib, Lily arose bright and early ready to greet the day. Bleary-eyed from travel and the flood of emotions at being reunited with her again, I pried myself out of bed and hurriedly dressed to allow my dad another hour of much-needed sleep. Even though it was only early October, I couldn't resist bringing an adorable pink cheetah costume I had bought her for Halloween. I put her in the costume, took her to the courtyard, and snapped a few pictures of her with the giant Agua volcano hovering in the background. I was trying to soak in as much of her infanthood as I could.

The beautiful courtyard was filled with colorful hammocks, a chilly, crystal blue in-ground pool, and gardens full of vibrant orchids and bougainvillea. As I thought about being a first-time mother, I had looked forward to so many things: our child's first smile, her first giggle, rolling over for the first time. At six months old I, however, I missed all of that. So when I visited, I tried desperately to savor all the milestones of Lily's babyhood I could.

An hour later my dad came out dressed in his blue chino shorts and plain white T-shirt. He had an air of leisure about him except that he was sporting his trusty yellow notepad, a government-issued black pen, dating back to his days as a supervisor at the US General Accounting Office in DC, and a few sections of the *Washington Post* newspaper he had brought from home. I guess he thought he would read his morning paper over breakfast. We made our way to the small terra-cotta patio where they were serving breakfast. It was an unusually quiet morning as there were no other tourists except a thirty-something, blond-haired woman drinking coffee alone at a large family-style table with a white triangle table cloth draped over it. Nearby was a little girl, whose age I couldn't quite make out. She appeared older than Lily and was scooting around in a brightly colored green walker. She squealed with delight as her thick curly black hair swooshed as she gained speed. I wondered if she was the blond woman's little girl. "Should I offer to sit down with her or take our breakfast to go?" I wondered. In such an intimate space, it seemed rude to just ignore her, so I asked, "Do you mind if we join you?"

"No, please do," she said, as she motioned to the chairs across from her. My dad and I sat down, placing Lily in a near-by plastic highchair as a waitress brought us glasses of fresh-squeezed orange juice.

The woman's name was Deb, and she was from Los Angeles, California. "LA, cool," I responded, as thoughts of a celebrity- and paparazzi-filled la-la land filled my head. "What do you do there?"

"Before coming to Guatemala to complete my daughter Pilar's adoption," she said motioning to the little girl rolling around happily in the walker, "I was Drew Carey's assistant. But once I get out of here, I'll probably stay home."

"Drew Carey as in the *Drew Carey Show?*"

She laughed. Because she was from LA, this was not a big deal to her, but to this East Coast girl, it was pretty impressive. She knew people. "Yeah, that Drew Carey."

I asked her how long her adoption process was taking.

"I've been at this for nearly two years; it's been a real struggle. I've been staying here at the hotel for a few weeks trying to resolve the issues I've had with getting Pilar's birth certificate. I've got a couple of connections, so hopefully I will have it in the next day or two. Then I'll finally be able to go back home to LA." While I didn't say anything, I knew that two years was a long time. The process was only supposed to take six to nine months' tops. It seemed like most people I met had smooth adoption processes, but then there were others like this woman and the woman at the Marriott who got stuck in an endless spider web of bureaucracy.

"I guess it's really helpful to have connections."

"Definitely," she said, taking a sip of her coffee. "We used this organization called Adoption Supervisors Guatemala."

I had read about them in an online chat room, but I hadn't actually met anyone using their services before. My dad pulled out his yellow legal notepad and wrote their name down. I love how my dad never wanted to miss a detail. He was always taking notes just in case someone might need a particular fact in the future.

"Their lawyers have been fantastic and helped us complete our adoption. We couldn't have done it without them. I highly recommend them."

As much as I appreciated the tip, I still couldn't help but think I wouldn't need their services.

Sadly, several days later, I had to leave Lily once again. Outside the airport, I unbuckled Lily from the out-of-date car seat proudly provided to us by our taxi driver and removed her from the retro 1970s car. I kissed her sweet head and said goodbye. I tried not to cry but did anyway. I glanced over at my dad. He wasn't one to show much emotion, but he too had big wet tears running down his face. "I'll be back soon, baby bean," I whispered as I handed her over to Camila and turned away quickly, feeling my heart being ripped out of my chest as I walked directly into the airport in the name of self-preservation.

Chapter 8

$\mathcal{I}$n the year since we had met the staff at Project Oz, so much had shifted. That November, our point of communication changed a third time. A cheerful woman named Dina would be serving as the new International Programs Director and would be taking over all the communications with the families to allow Karen to focus on the agency's administrative needs. While everything seemed legit, all this turnover was disconcerting.

While we had thought we would have Lily by now, because of the early issues with the DNA match, we still had a few more steps in the process. In mid-November, Dina called us. "I got word from the US Embassy last week," she said with excitement in her voice. "Your case has been approved, and Camila called me today and said your case has entered PGN."

PGN lawyers, also called reviewers, scrutinized the adoption paperwork to make sure everything was legit. If PGN approved your case, then you were legally approved by the Guatemalan authorities to adopt your child.

Like many adoptive parents, I stalked the online chat rooms to get a sense of how quickly PGN was processing cases. The majority of adoption petitions seemed to have a relatively smooth stay of four to eight weeks, with few to no kick-outs. A kick-out, also called a *previo*, could occur for a variety of reasons, such as spelling errors, an expired notary commission stamp, or a stamp on top of a signature. However, there were a few cases that ended up in PGN for twelve weeks or more. Those cases were flagged for irregularities and sent into investigations. This was adoptive parent hell; no one wanted to be there. Who knew if your case would ever come out approved or if the government authorities would terminate your case.

After hanging up with Dina, I assumed that our case was above board. I danced a happy jig in my office, twirling in a circle. "Thank you, thank you," I said gratefully. I figured we had nothing to worry about. Things were moving according to plan, and, Lord willing, Lily should be home in six to eight weeks.

Chapter 9

To celebrate my thirty-fifth birthday, my dad, my husband, and I traveled down again to Guatemala for my third, and hopefully, very last visit trip before Lily's adoption was finalized.

As we checked in to the Grand Tikal Hotel in Guatemala City, another place that was popular with prospective adoptive parents, I blinked in disbelief. Maria and Esteban, Lily's foster parents, were sitting on the dark leather sofa in the lobby with Lily, her hair in two little pigtails. But they were not supposed to be here for another hour with Camila.

I nudged Olav. "Hey, is that Maria and Esteban sitting over there?" I asked.

Olav looked discreetly over his shoulder. "Yep, that's them. I wonder what they're doing here so early."

We approached them gingerly, ecstatic to see Lily again. Lily was her usual joyful self. She crawled over the carpet on the marble floor and pulled herself up on the granite coffee table, banging her *pacha* (bottle) on the hard table. Maria rose to greet me. She kissed my cheeks and gave me a light embrace.

Maria cut right to the chase. Her eyes darted around the

lobby as she spoke. "Kim, I'm not receiving the things I need for Lily," she said. "Camila hasn't given me any money for food, diapers, or clothing. I am using all my own money to buy her these things."

After all the money we had given Project Oz, I was sure this couldn't be true. But we didn't care. We so wanted to do right by Lily. What was a hundred dollars to us? Nothing compared to what it would be worth to them.

Olav ran out of the hotel to find the nearest ATM. Twenty minutes later, he came back with 750 *quetzales*, the equivalent of approximately one hundred US dollars, and handed it to Maria. She took it gratefully and stuffed it into her bra.

"Kim, please keep in touch with us." There was something desperate in the way she spoke, though I wasn't sure why. "I can send you updates on Lily and pictures too." She reached into her jeans pocket and pulled out a small piece of paper with her e-mail address.

"Yes, we will." I was delighted to be able to have direct access to updates on Lily and not have to wait for Dina or Karen at Project Oz to fill me in.

Before I could get any more info on Lily, I heard the familiar sound of high heel shoes click-clacking on the tile floor. I turned to see Camila flanked by her brothers Juan and Manuel. Her face was red, and she immediately began scolding Esteban and Maria, wagging her brightly- painted red fingernail at them. The speed at which she was speaking made it difficult for me to comprehend, but her tone told me everything I needed to know. My face flushed with embarrassment for them as they slunk away out the door, not even looking back over their shoulder to say goodbye to their beloved Lily.

The next day, before our return flight back to the United States, we celebrated *El Día de Acción de Gracias* (Thanksgiving) in the Grand Tikal dining room surrounded by tourists, ex-pats, and well-to-do Guatemalans. We let Lily crawl all over the floor, entertaining our fellow dining patrons with her character and charm while we ate. I gave thanks to God for the bounty (which was a great contrast to what the majority of the people in Guatemala had) and our precious time together as a family. I also prayed fervently that we would be united as one on American soil shortly.

In typical Guatemalan fashion, the entire country shut down from mid-December to early January to enjoy the festive holiday season. At this point, Lily's case had been in PGN for only two weeks.

That Christmas, we joyfully prepared for her homecoming. I painted her room a creamy ivory, and Olav put together the white vintage crib we had been saving for years, just for this moment. The lovely butterfly duvet and matching curtains added just the right touch of pink, purple, and yellow to the room. We had received them from our family and friends at Lily's baby shower my sister threw just a few weeks earlier. My sister had been begging me for months to let her throw me a baby shower, but it wasn't until our case was in PGN that I finally felt that having a baby shower was sensible.

I hung up each of her little dresses and folded with care the petite onesies and diapers, all in anticipation of her arrival. I was nesting. Some nights I would tiptoe past her room as if she were already home sleeping and peek in offering up a silent prayer that her laughter—the thing I tended to remember most about Lily—would fill this sacred space soon.

As soon as the Guatemalan government reopened on January 3, I called Dina again to find out the status of our case. Lily had just turned ten months old. "No, nothing yet," she told me. "As far as I know your case is still in PGN, but I will definitely call you should Karen hear something." I had thought for sure she would be home by now. Since her case was still in PGN, Olav and I decided to revisit her. It would be my fourth time.

This time Camila arrived at the lobby of the Marriott hotel without the usual fanfare of her brothers or Lily's foster family. Lily happily was seated on Camila's slim hip. She greeted us with her infectious smile and delightful laughter. She had changed so much since we had seen her at Thanksgiving. She was chattering like a champ, pulling herself up on everything and anything. Socially, Lily was an equal opportunity lover. While I am not sure she recognized us yet, she was content to have just about anyone love on her.

I reached for Lily, and she nestled into my arms. I wanted to enjoy the moment, but the urgency of the situation distracted me. "It's been nearly six weeks now. Have you been able to check with Javier on our case now that PGN is back up and running?"

Her response came as a bit of a shock. "Javier's house burnt down last week, so he hasn't been able to go check on your file."

"Oh my gosh, that's terrible. Is he okay?"

"He's fine," she casually responded, as if an attorney's house burning down was an everyday occurrence in Guatemala. Maybe it was. It was odd, but I didn't give it too much thought.

After Camila left, Olav and I checked into our hotel room and began to unpack the new toys we brought for Lily. I pulled out a soft book filled with pictures of Lily and us from our last two visits, a play cell phone, and a stuffed Goofy that my friend had bought for Lily from Walt Disney World.

While we were unpacking the phone rang. I assumed it was Camila. I figured she had forgotten to tell us something. Instead, it was Maria. Her voice charged with emotion. "Kim, could we come to the hotel and visit Lily?" she asked.

"I-I-I, l-let me check," I stuttered, unsure of what to say. I knew they had been warned about having contact with us, but they were Lily's foster parents. I didn't feel like I could deny them that privilege. I asked Olav what he thought.

"I guess they are very attached to Lily," he said. "I suppose there is no harm in letting them come to visit. Anyway, who would know?"

The next day we met Maria and Esteban in the Marriott hotel lobby. Maria said, "*Hola mi niña*" (hello my little girl), as she rushed toward Lily and scooped her up in her arms. Esteban stood nearby patting Lily tenderly on her back. They obviously loved her as their own. I wondered if they wished they were the ones adopting her. Their deep attachment made me uneasy. I knew attachment was good for children, but I also knew that they would have a challenging time separating from Lily when the time came. If they couldn't even handle a short weekend away from her, how would they handle a lifetime? Hopefully things wouldn't be drawn out too much longer.

Twenty minutes into our visit, Olav grabbed my knee and whispered, "Look over there!"

I looked up, horrified, I clasped my hands over my gaping mouth. Manuel from Project Oz was in the hotel lobby, glaring at us. "You've got to go," I whispered to Maria and Esteban. They swiftly said their goodbyes and left. Manuel did not speak to us after they departed, but his grimace made it clear there would be consequences. How naïve we were to think that nobody would know of their visit.

Several days later, back in the lobby of the hotel, I handed Lily over to Camila, with Manuel standing watch nearby. I assumed Lily would go back home to Esteban and Maria. I worried about them slightly, but figured things would get sorted out. Little did I know we would never see them again.

Chapter 10

)J started feeling edgy as our time in PGN passed the critical six-week mark. I followed up with Karen, hoping for some reassurance. By now, I had the numbers at Project Oz memorized. "Camila mentioned that Javier's house had burned down and that he hadn't been able to check on our file. Is everything alright?" I asked.

"He seems to be fine. He's back at work," she said casually, as if having ones' house destroyed was not a major traumatic life event.

I took the hint to move on with my inquiry. "Any updates on our file?" I asked.

Her voice suddenly got serious. "Like I've told you before, your case continues to be in PGN. However, recently we have learned that we may have to pay a fifteen-hundred-dollar bribe to help expedite our cases."

"A what?" I said almost dropping the receiver in disbelief. This was so unethical. Sure, I knew bribes happened in shady practices, but it was never mentioned or outlined in Project Oz's payment schedule.

"I've never considered bribes before," Karen said, "but

Javier is telling me that the only way to expedite your case is to offer a bribe to the PGN reviewer next week."

A lump grew in my throat. "I'll... I'll... have to talk with Olav about that and get back to you."

Karen's tone was colder than she'd ever been before. "Just know if you decide not to pay the bribe, we can't guarantee how much longer your case will take."

I've always been such a naïve and trusting soul, assuming the best of people, but my faith in her was beginning to waiver. I did not like her nor her unethical business practices.

"By the way, Kim," she said as if talking about the weather. "Lily is no longer with Maria and Esteban." Even though Olav just put some wood in the stove and it was nearly seventy-five degrees in our home, my entire body got the chills.

"Where's my baby?" I asked, stunned at the revelation. Didn't they realize they were dealing with real live little human beings, not trades on Wall Street?

"Relax, Kim," she said coolly as though this were an everyday occurrence. "She's with a new foster mother named Vilma closer to Zone 10 in Guatemala City."

Relax! I didn't want to relax. My baby had been pulled out of the only home she had ever known, and this woman was telling me to relax!? Her children obviously had never been bounced around to different foster homes. And then Karen dropped another bomb on me. "Kim," she continued, "these foster families can be bad news. Sometimes they get too attached. Maria nearly ruined your adoption."

"What do you mean?" I asked. The reputation of consistent, loving foster care was one of the reasons we had chosen Guatemala. Sure, I had been nervous about their attachment to Lily, but they loved her.

"Maria called Lily's birth mother and told her to reconsider her adoption plan. She said we weren't looking out for Lily's best interests. You better be grateful to your attorney Javier, who reassured Lily's birth mother that he had everything under control." There was a stern tone to her voice as she added, "Remember, Kim, Lily is not your child yet. Her birth mother can change her mind at any time prior to her fourth and final sign-off of the adoption."

I couldn't believe this was happening. Six weeks earlier, I had been filled with so much hope. Now my daughter was in a new foster home, and we could lose her at any time during the process should her birth mother change her mind. As the truth of the situation began to sink in, I began cursing myself for our lapse in judgment. We should never have allowed Maria and Esteban to visit us at the hotel. How could we have been so foolish? No amount of deep breathing, Scripture, prayer, or Xanax could calm me down.

A few days later we received a desperate e-mail from Maria in very broken English. It read: "I do not know where Lily is. They did not return her to us. I am very worried about her. Camila, Manuel, and Juan do not care about the children. To them, they are just little bags of money. They never provided anything for her. I bought all her dresses and paid for all her medical care. I love her as if she were my own. Please, I am begging you. Please, hurry and take her away from these people because my heart is broken apart for Lily. Please contact me when you know where she is."

I turned away from the monitor and then hurled myself onto the untidy floor and cried out to God. "My strength is fading. I am no longer walking upright, trusting in you, but am crawling, face down in the dirt, barely hanging on." I opened my well-worn Bible, the one my mother gave me when I became a Christ-follower at the age of nineteen, and turned to book of Job. At that moment I felt like he was my kindred spirit, having also felt forsaken by God.

"What strength do I have that I should still hope? What prospects, that I should be patient? Do I have the strength of a stone? Is my flesh bronze?" (Job 6:11-12). My thoughts exactly.

Chapter 11

After twelve weeks in PGN, I was becoming unhinged. Something wasn't right. No one with "regular" adoptions went longer than twelve weeks. I called Project Oz again. "Just one more week," Karen said.

"I can't wait one more week," I said, clenching the phone tightly. I had already waited twelve weeks, and it was as if a sickness had spread through my body. I was infected, consumed. I had to know that Lily's case was not in investigations and that her case would be getting out of PGN soon.

"Kim, trust me," she said with a false sweetness in her voice. "I know it's hard to wait, but we are working on your case as quickly as possible." For a quick second, I regretted not paying that bribe, but then scolded myself for even considering it.

Posts on the Internet forums told of parents being able to call PGN directly to check on the status of their case. Others reported using an adoption supervisor service like the one Deb mentioned to me over six months ago, to check on the status of their case. I desperately wanted to do either of those things, but our legal contract with Project Oz explicitly forbade it. We were so in love with Lily, we didn't want to do anything else to risk losing her.

I called again. "Karen, I've read online that I can call PGN to check on my file. Is this true?"

Karen's response felt like a slap on the hand, "Kim, you've already caused enough trouble with Lily's foster parents and birth mother. *Do not* interfere with your case!"

I knew I shouldn't have pushed it any further, but I just had to know. "What about hiring an adoption supervisor? I've heard many people have used them successfully to check on their files."

Karen was now clearly exasperated with me. "The only person who can locate your case inside PGN is a PGN official. Rest assured your lawyer and Camila are checking at PGN daily for released cases, and they will contact me if they receive any news."

"Alright," I said, backing down. "I'll wait to hear from you."

Thirteen weeks... fourteen weeks... fifteen weeks... sixteen weeks... I called every week, and the excuses kept coming.

At sixteen weeks Karen said, "I'm sorry Kim, the attorney hasn't been able to check on the files this week. He's gone missing. Camila, Manuel, and Juan can't find him."

Just the week before Dina told us Javier was in a car accident and had burns on over 30 percent of his body. My self-restraint had been pushed to its limit. This couldn't be real. I couldn't wrap my brain around it. Everyone else was having normal stays in PGN. Not only was ours taking forever, but according to Project Oz, the attorney they hired to represent us was a constant victim of terrible circumstances.

Sheepishly I contacted Adoption Supervisors of Guatemala and inquired about their services. For a mere nineteen hundred dollars, they promised they would locate and validate an adoption case. It seemed like everyone was out to make a buck on ignorant Americans. I didn't want to be a fool anymore. I sent them the preliminary information they requested: Lily's full legal name, date of birth, and municipality of birth. But I didn't sign a contract and didn't give them any money yet.

Three days later, my phone rang. It was a man named Fernando, a lawyer with Adoption Supervisors Guatemala (ASG). "I received your inquiry regarding your adoption of the minor Lilian Rosmery Cajas Ramírez," he said. "I was able to go to PGN to check on the status of your file, I'm terribly sorry, but your paperwork was not there."

I almost dropped the phone. A lump began to grow in my throat. I hadn't expected that ASG would actually do anything with the information I sent them until I signed a contract. "How do you know that?" I asked, as I sat down on my rolling office chair.

"Kim, with the information you sent us I was able to go to PGN and do a computer search. When I didn't find it on the computer, I did a manual search in the special registration book where all the PGN entries are entered by hand. I even went to the civil registry to get a copy of Lilian's birth certificate to verify that I had the correct spelling. I'm sorry, but your case is not there."

I was nearly hyperventilating. "What do you mean our paperwork is not in PGN? Is our agency lying to us? Why did they tell us we had already finished Family Court in June prior to our first visit? We had to pay them half of our agency balance, and they even asked us for bribe money. I can't believe they would lie to us."

In spite of what he was telling me, Fernando's voice remained calm. "I know it's difficult to believe. Unfortunately, from my experience, there are a lot of unscrupulous people facilitating adoptions. Hence, the need for our services."

Olav and I had the very best of intentions. We felt like this was God's will for our life. It had never even occurred to me that people would try to profit off innocent children. I was learning that things were not always what they seemed.

"So what's next?" I asked.

"I went to Family Court to see if I could find your case. The good news is, it was there. I saw your dossier, and it was submitted to Family Court in December 2006 and assigned to a social worker. According to the social worker, they are simply waiting for the agency and its representatives to bring the birth mother and Lily to court, so they can interview them and hopefully sign-off one of the consents for the adoption."

My mind was racing. *This can't be,* I thought. *Project Oz had repeated many times that our case was in PGN with no issues. They even suggested we might consider paying a bribe to get our case out, and now Fernando at ASG was telling me that our case wasn't even in PGN, but was still in Family Court.* I was so conflicted. Who was telling the truth? I didn't know who or what to believe.

I tried to sound composed when I questioned Fernando as to how to proceed. "If what you are saying is true, and I can't let the agency know I am using your services, how do we advance our case without risking the entire adoption?"

"Tread very carefully," Fernando said. "Start by applying gentle pressure on your agency and their attorney to move the case forward."

I had no idea what he meant by applying gentle pressure. I felt so helpless.

"Kim, how much money have you paid them?"

"Twenty thousand dollars."

"As a consumer, you need to start demanding verification for services they claimed they have rendered. Call them and ask for the PGN entry receipt that they have so emphatically sworn to have in their possession."

I took a deep breath and exhaled slowly, the way my therapist had taught me to do when I felt overwhelmed. "Okay, I'll let you know how it goes."

"Please do," Fernando said. "And by the way, my assistant will send you the contract and money wire instructions via e-mail later today. Please sign it and arrange to have the money transferred."

Later that day, we received the contract. Even though ASG found our file, technically without our formal consent, I felt like we had to do something, so we signed the contract and sent off the money. I hoped I wasn't being foolish and that they could be trusted.

The next morning, as soon as the Project Oz office opened, I called Dina. Using an assertive, but polite voice, I said, "Lily is nearly twelve months old, and we have paid your agency twenty thousand dollars for services rendered. I don't think it is unreasonable to get proof of services executed. We will be visiting Lily next week, and I expect to have a copy of our PGN receipt by then."

"I'll have to talk to Karen," she said and then hung up the phone abruptly.

Chapter 12

It was the last week in March 2007, just a few days before Lily's first birthday, and once again Olav and I went to Guatemala. Project Oz had prohibited us from going on her actual birthday because it coincided with *Semana Santa*, or Holy Week, the week before Easter, which is one of the most elaborate and holiest celebrations in Guatemala, complete with grand processions, lavish floats, and intricately designed *alfombras* (carpets). The hotels would be packed, and travel would be made complicated by thousands of Guatemalans celebrating around the country. I had anticipated having her first birthday in the United States with friends and family, but Project Oz had different plans for us.

As we checked into the Marriott, the front desk clerk greeted us with familiarity. "Welcome back, Mr. and Mrs. Gjerde. Here to pick up your baby?"

"Sadly, no," I replied. "Just here to celebrate her first birthday."

"Well, let us know if we can do anything to make it special for you." How sweet! Even if we couldn't be with her on her actual birthday, it was nice to know that they would go out of their way to make it special for our family.

A few hours later, we heard the familiar sounds of Camila's pumps as she arrived through the back entrance of the Marriott hotel. Lily sat astride Camila's narrow hip, holding a half-drunk bottle of warm Nido brand milk. Olav, usually content to let me love on Lily first, reached for her, knowing that I had some business with Camila. Lily reached for Olav, dropping her bottle and bursting into laughter when she heard it hit the marble floor. Camila reached into her back pocket, and with a knowing grin on her face proudly handed me our receipt from PGN. I smiled and kept my face composed, so as not to reveal my total astonishment. I hadn't thought Karen would actually follow through, especially since she had empathetically told me many times that it was not policy to provide PGN receipts to adoptive families. I felt the strain of my neck muscles relax as Camila passed me the tiny little sheet of paper with a small black case number stamped on it. We had been in PGN all along. Project Oz had not been lying to us. I lifted up a silent prayer of thanks to God.

Two days later, we invited several other adoptive families whom we had met earlier in the day at the hotel to help us celebrate Lily's first birthday. "Please come, 2:00 p.m. later today, poolside, to help us celebrate Lily's first birthday." If we couldn't be surrounded by our friends and family back home, it would still be nice to celebrate this milestone with some other people.

I dressed Lily up in a frilly pink polka dot dress and pulled her hair back into two little pigtails and went downstairs to the pool deck. Through the help of the Marriott staff, I purchased a scrumptious tres leches cake covered with fresh whipped cream and strawberries. And then I waited. Olav and I sat in plastic lounge chairs for ten minutes, twenty minutes, then half an hour. No one showed up. I tried to make sense of it. You would think fellow adoptive parents would be kindred spirits and understand the value of celebrating milestones, but I guess everyone was busy.

Nearby two ladies, who we later learned were airline stewardesses for Delta, were having a drink.

"Excuse me," I asked, hoping I wasn't interrupting something important. "Do you mind joining us in singing happy birthday to our little girl? She will be one year old next week." I don't know why, but I desperately wanted someone else to share this joyful occasion with us.

"Of course," they replied in unison. "We'd be honored to."

With a single lit candle on the cake, we joined our voices and belted out "Happy Birthday" exuberantly followed by the Spanish version, "*Feliz Cumpleaños.*" My heart swelled with joy as we helped Lily blow out the candle.

While she sat in Olav's lap, I happily filmed her as she put all her tiny fingers in the cake; then lifted her fingers to her lips, tasting the deliciousness. She squealed in delight. She went back for more and then she proceeded to smear the whipped cream frosting from the cake all over her face, dress, and hair. She was adorable, savoring the sweetness of the cake to its fullest, just like she did life. Next, she proceeded to smear the whip cream frosting all over her daddy's face and clothing. Both of them were completely covered in icing as they howled with laughter. Even though her party wasn't what I had been anticipating, it was a precious sight.

———————————■———————————

Despite the tangible proof of the PGN receipt, I kept having nagging doubts. *Maybe I should send the PGN receipt to Fernando just to cover all my bases,* I thought. I walked down to the business center in the hotel and faxed him the receipt. Within minutes of sending the fax, Fernando called. "Sorry to disappoint you," he said, "but the receipt you sent me is not a PGN receipt but a PGN *previo.* It's given to people whose cases have been kicked out of PGN." The tension that had just left me a day ago returned.

"So if our case has been kicked out of PGN, what do we do now?"

"Kim, I know you don't want to believe me, but your case has never been in PGN. That *previo* belongs to another family. It's been doctored with your case number."

It was hard to believe that an adoption agency would go to the trouble to actually falsify documents. I wasn't sure what to believe anymore.

"I will bring you an example of an authentic PGN receipt tomorrow, so you can see for yourself." He lowered the tone of his voice in caution. "You must not speak of this false documentation to anyone. Any evidence of falsified documents will make your case a living nightmare." *As if it wasn't already.*

Upon our arrival home, I picked up the phone to call Project Oz. The phone rang one time. I heard, "We're sorry...you have reached a number that has been disconnected or is no longer in service." I must have misdialed. I put the phone receiver down and tried again. I dialed again, making sure to pound in each number with accuracy. I was greeted by the same message. Has their number really been disconnected? Maybe something was wrong with their phone lines? I sat down at the computer and sent off an e-mail to Project Oz, inquiring what was going on.

One day, two days, three days of complete silence and I was getting frantic. Many of us on the Project Oz Internet chat room speculated what could have possibly happened. Their phone lines went down? They didn't pay their phone bill? Or even worse, they went out of business without telling us.

Finally, after three long days, a group e-mail from Karen lit up my computer monitor. Karen's tone was businesslike, seemingly unaware of the mass panic her three-day absence had induced. "For your information, the contact number at Project Oz has changed. Our new contact number is (336) 841-6666. Furthermore, Dina has recently stepped down from her position as International Programs Director, and I will once again be the primary contact for your case."

My mouth gaped open. *First, Heidi resigns; then Karen steps up. Then Dina comes aboard and then resigns. And now Karen steps up again. Not to mention the three days of silence and the phone number change. What on earth was going on?* I thought.

I e-mailed her back immediately to inquire about the status of our case. She reported, "Your case was kicked out of PGN because of an error in the Family Court social worker's report, and now the social worker needs to re-interview Lily's birth mother and amend the report." I wondered if she was telling the truth or if that initial interview had never occurred as Fernando had said. It was a constant struggle knowing whom to trust. Catholic Charities had touted Project Oz as a reputable accredited adoption agency, but Project Oz's actions had severely damaged their credibility. While I didn't want to believe that Project Oz was lying to me, especially considering the large sum of money we had trusted them with, I suspected that Fernando had been telling us the truth all along. We had never been in PGN as Karen and Dina at Project Oz had blatantly claimed, but our case had been stuck in Family Court waiting for the birth mother to be interviewed.

Two weeks later, Karen told us that the repair had been made to the Family Court report and that our case had been resubmitted to PGN. I was pleased with myself; all my pressure was finally paying off. I ran into the kitchen where Olav was cooking dinner to share the good news. "Looks like Lily's case is finally moving forward."

Reluctant to take Karen at her word any longer, Olav suggested I call Fernando to confirm.

"Definitely!" I said, "I'll call him first thing tomorrow morning."

The next morning, I called Fernando, and he said he would look into it. Two days later, he followed up, "I'm sorry to report there has been no birth mother interview at Family Court or submission to PGN, as Project Oz has claimed." What a fool I was. Why did I even think they could be telling the truth? When was I going to learn to stop being so trusting?

Chapter 13

April 3, 2007 was Lily's first birthday. Nearly one year into the adoption process and our case was no further along than it had been five months earlier. For me, it magnified a year of loss. I had missed her first time rolling over, sitting up, crawling, hearing the heart-melting sounds of her first "mama" or "dada." I spent the day in a teary haze. I couldn't help but rehash the drama of the past twelve months: the continual lies and incompetence of Project Oz, the loss of Lily's first foster family, and the fear of jeopardizing her adoption that constantly haunted me.

By May 2007, I was on a mission to determine the truth once and for all. I took a deep breath, trying to reign in the rising emotion in my chest, and called Karen. "I expect verification of all the actions you and your Project Oz staff have claimed to have done. I want to see a copy of my resubmitted PGN receipt as well as a copy of our completed Family Court report."

"Okay, Kim," Karen replied, trying to pacify me. "I'll have Camila and Manuel bring them to you when they drop off Lily."

That month I boarded a plane for the sixth time and traveled once again down to Guatemala with my dear friend Elaine, a former roommate from my single days and a faithful prayer warrior. I was so thankful for her willingness to support me on my mission. I was determined not to leave Guatemala until I knew the truth; my sanity depended on it.

Lily's new foster mother, Vilma, a slender, affable older woman with short wavy gray hair that reeked of cigarette smoke, was waiting for us at the entrance of our new hotel in Antigua along with her eight-year-old granddaughter. Vilma appeared to have a grandmotherly affection for Lily, which was a nice contrast to the intense protectiveness of Maria. The moment Lily's eyes met mine, her face lit up, and she tottered quickly over to me as Vilma held her hand to help her keep her balance. She stretched out her arms to me, as if to say, "Mama, I've missed you."

Vilma exclaimed, "She knows you!"

My heart melted. Lily wrapped her sweet baby arms around my neck as I lifted her up and kissed her sweet angelic face. It made all six visit trips worth it!

Standing nearby was Manuel who was holding a large brown envelope, which I suspected contained the receipts I had demanded. Before he and Vilma left the hotel, he handed over the envelope. "Everything you requested should be in there," he said.

As soon as they left, I peeked inside the envelope, hoping that everything would be in order. Before our departure, I had sent Karen an e-mail specifying the documents I wanted. Inside were only two of the four items I had requested. *What is wrong with these people?* I wondered if the documents were even legit. I faxed everything to Fernando to verify their validity.

Half an hour later, Fernando called me. "I'm sorry, Kim," he said when he called. "These receipts are missing the essential information that makes them valid. The one PGN receipt doesn't include a case number or a date, and the Family Court document is full of obvious errors. Call your agency and let them know." I couldn't believe they were doing this to me. If blood could boil, mine was about to spill over and leave a big mess. I had to use every iota of self-control to prevent myself from spewing forth venomous wrath at Karen when I called her.

This time my voice was unusually forceful and confrontational. "I am sick and tired of paying for services and not getting any credible proof. I want valid paperwork sent immediately."

She must have known I meant business, because the next day, she sent scans of new documents via e-mail without an argument. Once again, I forwarded them to Fernando in hopes that he would confirm their validity.

"Sorry, Kim," he said, his voice tinged with sympathy. "These documents do not belong to your case. They belong to another family." I was going to implode. It's one thing to lie once, but it's another thing to continue to lie. Did they think we were idiots? Did Karen and Camila believe their own lies?

There was nothing I could do except continue to apply

gentle pressure while Fernando calmly reminded me to keep my cool. Whether I liked it or not, Karen and Camila held all the strings, and if I pushed them too far, I could jeopardize Lily's adoption.

Two days later Fernando called, "I have made an appointment for you on Monday at 9 a.m. to go to Family Court. There you will be able to see your documents, talk directly to the social worker involved in the case, and find out what specific steps are needed to pass through Family Court.

"Super," I replied. I couldn't wait.

Sunday night before the appointment, I woke up with a start and bolted to the bathroom, making it just in time. The tortillas from the street vendor the night before obviously were not agreeing with me. *Not now! Of all the days for my stomach to be my Achilles heel.* By six the next morning, I was still lying beside the toilet, weak and exhausted from hours of vomiting and a lack of sleep. I hoped I would be able to make it through the day without causing a scene.

As I caught a taxi down to Fernando's office in the city, I hoped and prayed that my body would stop revolting.

At 9 a.m. Fernando and I walked together into Family Court No. 7. It reminded me of a state-run old-folks' home or a severely neglected elementary school on the wrong side of the tracks. The harsh fluorescent lights illuminated the broken tile floor and aged yellow walls. A nice coat of bright white paint would have cheered the place up. The hallway had a stale smell, like the windows to the outside had been painted shut. Fernando strode with an air of confidence toward a small wood-paneled desk. He had obviously been here many times before. A social worker known to me as only social worker No. 1 sat behind a desk stacked with papers.

Social worker No. 1 smiled politely as she showed me a copy of our incomplete Family Court report.

"Lily's birth mother is supposed to come in today at 11:00 a.m. for her interview," Fernando translated, as the vocabulary of Family Court was a few notches above my basic conversational Spanish.

I was not content with just words. I wanted solid evidence. I wanted to see the final social worker report. "How will I know the interview has occurred and what certification will you put on the report to validate its authenticity?"

"Someone from your agency should call you later today to confirm," she said through Fernando as she showed me a set of three stamps that had to be placed on the document for it to be official. "Just so you know," the social worker told me, "I've had this file on my desk since December, and I have simply been waiting for the birth mother to come in." I supposed she didn't want to be blamed for Project Oz's incompetence.

I thanked her for her time and then Fernando and I departed Family Court.

An hour later, Karen called me and reamed me out. "What the hell were you doing at Family Court? If you mess up your case, I am washing my hands of you."

I was tired of being polite. Without meaning to, the rage spewed out of me. "I'm sick and tired of the lies and the false documentation. We've paid your agency a ton of money for your services. I want the truth."

Karen promptly made a phone call to Camila so we could have a three-way phone conversation. Camila stammered in Spanish, apologizing profusely. "I will take you to Family Court this afternoon to sort everything out," she said.

Later that day, I returned to Family Court with Camila. This time I brought Lily and an independent translator. I don't know why I was surprised, but the story changed from my earlier visit. Social worker No. 1 was obviously in cahoots with Camila and was doing everything in her power to help cover her tracks. "Of course, Lily's birth mother was interviewed back in April 2006 shortly after Lily's birth. I must have been mixed up Lily's birth mother with another woman."

Every time the social worker opened her mouth, she shared another piece of contradictory information. "Lily's file must have gotten lost when social worker No. 2 quit her job in July. It wasn't found until this past December, and it has been sitting on my desk ever since."

"July?! You just told me a minute ago that Lily's birth mother was interviewed back in April." By now my head was pounding. "What about the stamps you mentioned earlier. If Lily's birth mother was interviewed, where are those stamps?"

She continued to perjure herself, "This," she said, motioning to the incomplete social work report, "is only a copy. The official Family Court document with the stamps is in PGN with your dossier."

As accommodating as the social worker had been earlier

in the day, it was apparent that she was now lying shamelessly to protect Camila. I finally realized beyond a shadow of a doubt that Karen and Camila could no longer be trusted.

If being queasy and having a case of the runs all day wasn't bad enough, that evening, I developed a case of full-body hives. Thank goodness Elaine had been there to care for Lily during my malaise. I would not have survived the trip without her support.

The next day, for the first time ever, I boarded the plane, eager to leave Guatemala. I was mentally and emotionally drained. I was running on empty.

Two weeks later, I tried to plan another trip to visit Lily. Karen wouldn't even return my phone calls, but sent me a brazen e-mail saying, "Because of all the trouble **YOU** have caused, the attorney has forbidden you from visiting Lily until the adoption has been completed."

Attorney!? What attorney? I had tried to meet with Javier when I was down in Guatemala a few weeks ago and was told by Manuel that the attorney could not meet with me because his house burned down (for the second time!), he was in a car crash and had to get treatment, and that he had to take his mother somewhere because she was sick. It was one excuse after another so that I would never meet this man. I realized that even though Javier was our attorney of record, he was just a cheap unscrupulous lawyer who sold his rubber stamp to Project Oz in order to process their cases through the system. I screamed and cried into my pillow until I collapsed on my bed in exhaustion. This was so unfair, and yet all I could do was wait. We were at the mercy of Karen and Camila.

Toward the end of June, over nineteen months since the process had started, we received a friendly e-mail from Karen. She seemed to be singing a different tune. "Your case has been submitted to PGN and attached is a valid PGN receipt." Who was this woman? An informative e-mail and a PGN receipt without me demanding it. I could hardly contain my enthusiasm.

I ran out to the living room like a crazy person waving a printout of the e-mail and the PGN receipt in Olav's face, as he was trying to unwind with a glass of red wine on the couch. "Did you send it to Fernando to verify it?"

An hour later, Fernando responded, "Great news, Kim. It's legit. Your case is officially in PGN." I was thrilled! It had been a long road, but assuming all our paperwork was in order, we would only have to wait for another four to eight weeks before she should be coming home.

I was flying high, but then I came crashing down again when, eighteen days later we learned that our case had been kicked out with seven trivial errors in the paperwork that would need to be corrected by Javier, our Guatemalan "attorney" and then need to be resubmitted to PGN by Camila. I was so mad at myself for being so naïve, thinking that our case would fly through PGN without any issues. It had taken us over fourteen months for Lily's referral to be submitted to PGN the first time. Who knew when we would ever be resubmitted?

A doer by nature, I needed to do something to escape, before I spiraled even further. Some people drink or do drugs to escape their reality. I traveled. In my twenties and early thirties, I traveled overseas independently, backpacking to many different countries in Europe, South America, and Asia. It was my happy place. Nothing made me feel more alive, joyful, and free than trekking around exploring new places and meeting new people.

While Olav didn't like the idea of me traveling alone, he also understood my need to escape, so we compromised. I would travel to Spain with an escorted group tour for ten days. In mid-July, I packed my bags and headed off to Spain. My prayer was that when I returned, our case would be resubmitted to PGN.

Spain was a wonderful escape. In Barcelona, I leisurely strolled down Las Ramblas and visited the Roman Catholic church Sagrada Familia. In Madrid, I sat with some fellow tourists in the Plaza Mayor, a famous city square, enjoying a pitcher of sangria. In Granada, I visited the UNESCO World Heritage site, the Alhambra. Nevertheless, Lily's situation still haunted me daily. While in Spain, I had one of my new friends, a fellow tourist and native Spanish speaker, call Camila on my behalf. I was tired of dealing with Karen, and after all my trips to Guatemala, I knew that Camila was the primary one doing the paperwork in Guatemala anyway. I was hoping to hear some promise of our case moving forward, but unfortunately, the news was not good. Our case had not been resubmitted at all. There was no escaping the sadness. It was like a dark shadow that followed me everywhere.

Upon returning from Spain, we received a formal letter in the mail from Project Oz. "We are sorry to inform you, but the Maryland Project Oz office will be closing down permanently effective July 31, 2007. We know you may have concerns, but have no fear, Karen, who has been your primary point of contact, will continue to oversee your case from the corporate offices in North Carolina."

I assumed the last sentence was supposed to be a comfort to us, but I found it anything but comforting. Project Oz was leaving the state of Maryland, Karen and her team were compulsive liars, and our case didn't appear as if it would ever be resubmitted to PGN anytime soon. I couldn't just sit around waiting. I had to do something.

Chapter 14

*C*ut off from visiting Lily, unable to receive honest and ac-
curate information from Karen, and with the Maryland
office closing down, Olav and I felt like we needed to hire an
attorney to help us navigate this hellhole on the domestic side.
Through an Internet search, we found an accredited adoption
lawyer named Jennifer Fairfax. Though her experience was
primarily in domestic adoption, she was willing to use her
creativity to help us apply pressure to our adoption agency in
a professional yet assertive way. With her assistance, we were
able to procure visitation rights to Lily again in October 2007.

Once again, we checked into the Marriott Hotel. Camila
arrived holding Lily's hand as she toddled in with a look of
confidence on her face. Manuel and Juan stood beside her like
scrawny bodyguards. Juan had a tough, street-smart sense
about him, but Manuel was more like a grunt laborer, doing
exactly what Camila told him to do. "Look at our girl walking,"
I exclaimed, grabbing Olav's arm in excitement. Six months
ago in May, when I saw her last, she would take a step or two
and then fall. Now she was practically running.

I wasn't sure if Lily would remember me, but she ran right

up to me, eager to be enveloped in a big hug. However, my joy was short-lived as soon as Camila began to speak. "We haven't told Vilma yet," she said. "But Lily is going to a new foster home after your visit. Vilma has been selling Lily's name-brand Nido milk and giving her the cheap stuff." *Right, I'm sure*, I thought to myself. If anything, Vilma was lucky if Camila was even giving her money for Lily's milk. Even though I was confident they were lying, it didn't change the disturbing reality that Lily was going to change her foster home for the third time in less than eighteen months. Poor Lily already had the initial loss of her birth mother and her first foster family. That meant if we ever gained custody of Lily, we would be her fourth home. A child shouldn't have to endure that. This was incredibly cruel.

But it gave me an idea. "I can't stand the thought of Lily changing foster homes again. Would it be possible for me to stay here in Guatemala and foster Lily until the completion of the adoption?" I asked. I knew I should have talked to Olav first and prayed about it before I opened my mouth, but as any mother knows, sometimes you just have to go with your gut. Thankfully my husband's jaw did not drop. In fact, it was like he read my mind.

A few weeks earlier, Fernando shared that Camila's relationship with Karen had become increasingly strained. In a different adoption case at ASG, Camila had agreed to keep their relationship confidential from Project Oz and work cooperatively with ASG to help move the case forward. I hoped that Camila might be willing to agree and go behind Karen's back. Still, I did not expect Camila to agree so readily, but she did.

"That would be excellent," she said. I assumed she cleverly realized that it would take Lily off her bankroll. "I just need a thousand dollars to pay the attorney, and then I can get your case in and out of PGN in six weeks. But you must promise not to tell Karen." I had no idea how she would manage to do that, but I didn't care. I was finally going to be with Lily. I swore up and down that I would not mention our arrangement to Karen, and I'd figure out how to come up with the thousand dollars later.

It turned out Manuel seemed to have a soft spot for me. He said, "Kim, please come live with my family in our home. I have room for you and Lily." I don't know why he offered to help me, but perhaps he hoped that by helping me, I might help him and his family get to the USA one day. After all, I had learned that every American was a wealthy meal ticket to many Guatemalans. I had wanted to move to Antigua, but I didn't feel like I could say no.

The next day I called my work to let them know I would be taking my maternity leave immediately. While I couldn't see his face, I am pretty confident that my administrator was as shocked as I was.

Two days later, I climbed into that rusted red beat-up Datsun and held Lily on my lap. The door clanked shut. I waved goodbye to Olav as the engine coughed to life and we took off. Holding back tears and putting on a brave, stoic face, I watched my husband fade into the background as we barreled forward onto the bumpy road. I felt like I had stepped onto a high wire with no safety net below. Unbeknownst to me, we were headed to Villa Nueva, one of the most gang-ridden neighborhoods in Guatemala.

From the exterior, Manuel's barrio looked more like a correctional facility than a neighborhood. It was surrounded by tall concrete walls with razor-sharp barbed wire and broken glass on top. A private security guard wielding a pump-action shotgun checked our IDs and then went over the car with a telescoping inspection mirror. After seven visits to Guatemala, I was somewhat numb to this normal cultural phenomenon, as all the gated neighborhoods had controlled access points.

The self-contained neighborhood had a small play park; a well-loved soccer field and basketball court; several little hole-in-the-wall *tiendas* selling essentials such as milk, tortillas, and eggs; and a makeshift Internet café. Except for work, there was no reason to leave the heavily patrolled compound.

Manuel and Graciela's home was a basic cinder block row home with two bedrooms and one bath, painted a warm sunny yellow. Compared to some of the corrugated metal shanty shacks I had seen in Guatemala, their house was a palace. Manuel offered Lily and me one of his bedrooms which had a queen-size bed and a hand-carved armoire, which had a mirror and a shelf. For drapes, there was a threadbare piece of fabric hung in front of the window for privacy. I knew this was a sacrifice for them. After all, four people, including Manuel and his wife, would all share a queen-size bed in the next room.

The next morning, after Manuel and Graciela left for work, my initiation to life in Villa Nueva began. Yolanda, Manuel's sister-in-law, also lived in the house and her job was to care for Manuel and Graciela's son, Alejandro, who was eight months younger than Lily. Yolanda and I took the kids to the park in the center of the neighborhood compound. Lily and Alejandro took turns shrieking with glee on the blue Little Tykes baby swing. After a short time, we headed back to the house to do some cleaning before getting ready for lunch. Turning the key to the door, I entered first. Immediately I noticed that the back door from the kitchen to the enclosed dirt backyard was wide open. I could have sworn I double-checked the locks before we left, but maybe I forgot to close it all the way. I walked gingerly to the back door and checked the lock. It was fully intact; there was no sign of forced entry. I began to look around the kitchen and noticed other things were off. The already sparse kitchen was even more barren: the double propane camping stove that they cooked on and the small refrigerator were gone.

A sense of alarm overtook me. "Yolanda, I think we have been robbed."

She stared at me in disbelief, frozen in the doorway with the two kids. In hindsight, I should have been more cautious as I walked in. The thieves could still have been inside the house, but my brain couldn't process the situation fast enough.

"Look," I beckoned her as I scanned the living room. "The shelf is empty."

Manuel's prized possessions, his old, beat-up boom box, which the entire family used daily, and their beloved thirteen-inch black-and-white television set, which got three fuzzy channels with its duct-taped rabbit ears, were gone. I called Yolanda out of her stupor and told her to go check the other bedroom. I walked into my bedroom. The few items of clothing I had brought with me were thrown carelessly on the bed. My small navy blue wallet was open and pillaged. My various credit cards were strewn about, and the little bit of cash I had was gone. Miraculously, my passport was left untouched. The knapsack I'd brought, which contained my pre-paid cell phone, my only line to the outside world, and my iPod and video camera, which contained all the pictures and videos from Lily's first birthday, was gone. All tangible evidence of Lily's first milestones was gone.

Yolanda checked the other room and reported that everything appeared to be intact. It was obviously an inside job, a total set up. After all, this was a gated community with controlled access. Someone had been watching us, just waiting for the little rich *gringa* to leave so they could ransack the house. It unnerved me to think about what would have happened to us had we come home in the middle of the robbery. Surely God's hedge of protection was with us.

In Guatemala, many people distrust and fear the police. They are widely dismissed as inefficient, corrupt, and abusive, so Yolanda wasn't about to call them for help. She spent hours trying to reach Manuel and his family on their cell phones. Despite the unsettledness of the day, Yolanda continued her daily routine as if nothing unusual had occurred. I helped out the best I could, hiding my uneasiness while mopping the white tiled floors and watching Lily and Alejandro. I was wracked with guilt. If I hadn't been staying there, this never would have happened.

As Yolanda prepared dinner, Lily, Alejandro, and I were outside playing with a plastic orange ball that I had bought the day before from one of the street vendors in the compound. Manuel, along with his entire extended family, arrived together to survey the losses. A crime against one member of the family was a crime against all. Suddenly I became confused when several black pick-up trucks with sirens blaring and lights flashing converged on the scene. Dozens of men in black flak jackets and with M16 assault rifles jumped out of the back of the cab. It was like a scene from a movie.

I heard Manuel, usually non-confrontational, shouting at the cops. The neighbors, who had been sitting outside enjoying the coolness of the evening, began to scurry inside, fearing for their safety. Camila, who stood nearby, glanced over at me and then to Lily. Realizing the danger of the situation, she commanded two neighboring Guatemalans to usher Lily away, since Lily's foster mother of record was still Vilma. There were rumors of foreigners stealing children—either to adopt or, in the more fantastic versions, to harvest their organs for transplants—which caused several American women to be lynched or nearly beaten to death. An American woman found with an undocumented child could be calamitous.

Before I was aware of what was happening, Manuel led me indoors and shoved me into the cramped bathroom and ordered me to remain silent and hide behind the toilet. The toilet smelled of urine and lingering excrement. I curled into a fetal position in the narrow space behind the commode and closed my eyes tightly. I felt like I was going to vomit. I began to pray silently. "God the threat outside is so great, please, God, I beg you, don't give the police any reason to search this room. Please place an army of angels around Lily." Suddenly, I heard a rifle cock as the sound of combat boots struck the tile floor next to the closed bathroom door. I was trembling, sweat was dripping down my back, and my calf muscles were screaming out in pain. I wanted to sit down and squeeze myself even smaller behind the porcelain john, but the fear of making any noise paralyzed me. I sucked in my breath so as not to be heard.

For about an hour, time stood completely still. Words drifted under the door. I strained my ears to catch bits and pieces of the conversation, but none of it made any sense. There was too much commotion. At last, the loud and forceful voices of the cops faded away. I slowly unfurled my clenched body. Finally, there was a light rap on the door. "Kim," Camila whispered. "You can come out now. The police are gone."

Sore and exhausted, I came out of the bathroom and saw Lily playing with a basket of toys in the living room, oblivious to all the trauma. I rushed toward her, scooped her up in my arms, pressed her tightly to my body, and lifted up a silent prayer of thanks to Jesus.

That night sleep did not come easily. I kept thinking someone was outside watching me, planning to break in again by shattering the unbarred window to my room. I was a vulnerable target with nothing to protect me.

The next morning, Manuel went out to purchase iron bars for the windows, and I told Camila, "You have to get me the legal foster parent papers for Lily immediately."

"Yes, Kim, I will take care of that first thing tomorrow morning," she said. And for the first time ever, she was true to her word.

Chapter 15

After seventy-two hours in Villa Nueva, Camila came over for a visit. We gathered around the dining room table. I pulled up one of the wooden chairs anticipating what new information she needed to share with me. "Kim, your paperwork can't return to PGN because most of the documents in your dossier have expired," she told me.

"Expired?" I didn't even know the documents could expire. With the exception of waiting longer than usual for the adoption to go through, our status quo hadn't changed. We both had the same jobs, we hadn't moved, we continued to be healthy, we hadn't committed any crimes, and as far as I knew our fingerprints hadn't changed.

"I just learned myself, but apparently the state of Maryland, the United States Immigration Department, and the Guatemalan government require this information to be updated every twelve to fifteen months, depending on which agency is involved."

I couldn't believe it. We had paid Project Oz thousands of dollars to guide us through this maze, and now we had to start all over again.

Camila patted me on the arm. "Lily can stay with my aunt while you take care of things in the States." I had heard about this aunt on the Project Oz Internet chatrooms. A few other adoptive parents had mentioned that their child was pulled out of their foster homes and placed with another woman known as Camila's aunt. I assumed it was Camila's attempt to pocket foster care money for herself.

What could I do? I had to go home and get this paperwork done, and someone had to take care of Lily. And it wasn't like Camila was giving me a choice. I was going to have to trust that Lily would be okay and that I would be able to get back to her as quickly as possible.

We drove to Camila's aunt's house on the morning of my departure. I wanted to cry, but I held it in. I didn't want Lily to sense my apprehension and fear. I had promised Lily I would never leave her again and yet here I was leaving her with another unknown caretaker.

We pulled up in front of the aunt's house. Manuel and Graciela's house was a mansion compared to this place. The door swung open and Camila's aunt came out to the concrete slab porch to greet us.

"*Bienvenidos, pasen adelante,*" (Welcome, come in) she said with enthusiasm, as she motioned for us to enter the house.

I walked in warily, securely holding Lily in my arms and taking it all in. As I entered, I immediately noticed the corrugated metal roof over our heads and a damp, musty smell. They must have had some serious issues with water during the rainy season. We passed by the "living room," which was littered with various electronics equipment I could not identify. It appeared as if someone had been dumpster diving and simply strewn their findings on the floor.

Camila's aunt introduced me to her husband who was lying shirtless on a 1970s brown checkered couch. Barely taking his eyes off his small rabbit-eared television, he took a sip of his beer and greeted me with a nod. I couldn't believe I had to leave Lily in this dump.

Camila's aunt pulled back the threadbare cloth separating the living room from the bedroom where Lily would be sleeping. The bedroom was equally as cluttered with more electronic components, stuffed animals, random toys, and clothing strewn about. It looked like a bomb had gone off and sent debris flying. In the corner of the disheveled room was a small brown cradle, which was filled with more paraphernalia.

"This is where Lily will sleep," she said assuredly.

I did my best to hide my awful thoughts and gave her a weak but encouraging smile. *If Lily doesn't strangle herself on all the clutter in the house, I swear she will suffocate to death in the crib*, I thought.

"I promise I'll take good care of her for you, just like my own babies."

"Gracias," I said faintly, as I passed Lily over to her. *Keep moving*, I thought. *This is Guatemala. Things are different here. She will be all right.*

My first full day back in the States was overwhelming. The

tasks ahead seemed insurmountable. We were basically start-ing all over again. I was determined to do my very best to get things done, but I knew what I was up against. Our initial adoption paperwork had taken over five months.

First, I called Adoptions Together, a local and well-re-spected adoption agency that Jennifer Fairfax, our domestic adoption attorney, had recommended we contact to get our home study updated. On the first ring, a cheerful social work-er by the name of Anna answered the phone. As I explained the situation, Anna took pity on me. "I just happen to have a cancellation," she said. "Would I be able to come out to your house mid-week to do a walk-through and interview both you and your husband?"

"That would be incredible," I said. I couldn't believe it. So-cial workers normally scheduled home studies months in ad-vance and this woman was willing to come out in a matter of days.

"As soon as you get all your clearances, I should be able to turn around your updated home study report pretty quickly." I had never been big into angels, but I was convinced this woman was heaven-sent. I couldn't shake the feeling that God's hand was in all of this. While I had asked my friends to pray when I came home, it was a half-hearted gesture. I didn't really expect that God would answer their prayers on my be-half. I figured it would have been all up to me to work these things out, and yet God was removing obstacles I had abso-lutely no control over.

My second day in the States, I went online to schedule an appointment at the US Immigration office in Baltimore. I clicked on the appointment screen and my face lit up. The last time I tried to do this, I had had to wait for over a month. Now I saw a single appointment block available for both paperwork and fingerprints later in the week. It was like the red carpet was being laid out just for me.

The next day, I felt God's presence as He continued to open door after door. When I walked into the police station, a stern grey-haired officer greeted me in the lobby. As I explained my situation, his demeanor softened. He was no longer a tough cop but a loving father wanting to help a fellow parent. "I can help you," he said. "I have a grown son, the light of my life, whom we adopted from Korea many years ago."

The same thing happened at the doctor's office. When I went for my updated physical, Dr. Stark mentioned that she too had an adopted daughter from China and remembered with nostalgia the days of trying to get all the paperwork in order. Both the officer and the doctor presented my completed paperwork within an hour, as if they had my information on file in some backroom somewhere. I literally skipped out of the doctor's office and police station with my paperwork in hand.

I was giddy with excitement, eager to share the good news with Olav when I got home. Olav, in a rare display of unrestrained emotion, jumped up and down with me, like we were two little kids receiving the news that we were going to Walt

Disney World for Christmas. We couldn't believe that God had moved all those insurmountable mountains in only a week, so I could return to Guatemala and be with Lily again.

Chapter 16

After my one week in the States, Camila and her brother Juan met me at the airport with Lily in tow. I ran to her and scooped her up, delighted that she appeared well. She shrieked with laughter as I planted kisses all over her sweet little head. It was like I had never left. We hopped in the car and returned to Manuel and Graciela's house in Villa Nueva.

As the weeks passed in Villa Nueva, I began to feel suffocated. Trapped. Every morning Graciela and Manuel left to go to work, and Yolanda and I didn't go anywhere. We passed the long hours trying to communicate with my mangled Spanish, entertaining the kids, going to the park, and doing chores. We swept and mopped the floors in the sparse house and washed clothes and dishes in the outdoor *pila* (a concrete basin with a scrub board attached). We hung the clothes up to dry for a few hours before the afternoon rains came. Then we had to take them down until the rain passed only to have to rehang them again when the clouds cleared. Yolanda never complained, but to me it felt like a prison sentence without a parole date.

In addition to my increasing cabin fever, life inside the neighborhood compound was becoming problematic for me.

Nearly every day when I would go outside for a walk to get some fresh air, I would hear the neighborhood men, who sat on their front steps drinking beers, calling out to me, "*Oye mami, guapa*" (Hey, pretty mama) while grabbing their crotches and gesturing at me. I could hear their drunken laughter as I walked past. I knew they were just trying to rile me up. Considering the robbery three weeks earlier and the lack of other people around, I was uneasy, afraid they might leap off their steps and harm me. Pushing Lily in her stroller, I walked briskly past them, pretending not to hear their snide remarks.

One day when pushing Lily down the street in her stroller, a young woman, who appeared several years younger than me, began walking beside me. In broken English she said, "Hello, I'm Melany. Are you American?"

I was surprised by her boldness as most Guatemalan's I had met were not very forthright. "Yes, I am from Maryland, right outside of Washington, DC."

The woman explained that she had lived and worked in Brooklyn for several years before moving back to Guatemala.

Returning her friendliness, I asked, "Is that where you learned your English?"

She flashed a proud smile and said, "Yes, I had taken English classes here in Guatemala, but it didn't really prepare me for the English in the States."

I laughed in agreement. "Tell me about it," I said. "That's how I feel about my Spanish. I took four years of Spanish in school, but I still can't speak in sentences."

She giggled like a teenage girl. I liked her. She was sweet

and seemed genuinely interested in me. Over the next few days, whenever I was out walking with Lily, she would come outside to walk beside me. Being away from everything familiar, it was a pleasant distraction to speak English to someone else and have a person outside of Yolanda and the kids to talk to each day.

Two weeks later, she invited me over for a meal. Leaving Lily at home with Yolanda, I walked down the block to her house. After being with Lily 24/7, it felt liberating to go out for some much-needed adult time. As I entered Melany's house, I noticed the typical red-and-white checkered plastic table cloth covering the wooden table with the picture of the Virgin Mary hanging proudly above it on the otherwise bare pale yellow walls. She offered me a seat and brought out some chicken pepián, a traditional Guatemalan spicy stew, and a glass of ice, cold Coca-Cola.

We made small talk and just as I was about to take a bite into the chicken she said, "My uncle is sick. I don't have any money to help him. Can you help me?"

It was as if she had practiced this spiel many times before. I put the fork down, closed my eyes momentarily, and took a deep breath. I had thought I had made an actual friend, but in reality, I was just a piggy bank.

"I'm sorry I can't help you," I said. I stood up and thanked her for the food, turned on my heels, and walked out the door.

Back at Graciela and Manuel's house, things were getting

troublesome. Like many men in Guatemala, Manuel began to drink away his daily paycheck, sometimes disappearing for days, only to come home to play soccer and then disappear again. Graciela was making only 893 *quetzales* (about $120) every other week for over ninety hours of labor. (I learned this because Lily accidentally pulled out one of her check stubs while we were cleaning.) She frequently asked me for money and food since Manuel was no longer providing for his family. While I was thankful for their hospitality, I wanted out of Villa Nueva.

One evening when Camila and Juan dropped Manuel off at home for a soccer game, I pulled Camila and Manuel aside. "My dad called earlier today on Yolanda's phone," I told them. "He is worried sick about me and doesn't like the idea of me living in Guatemala. He'll be at the Grand Tikal Hotel by the end of the week to stay with me until the completion of Lily's adoption."

The truth was that my dad was coming to visit but not for another two weeks, and he sure wasn't staying until the end of the process. My conscience screamed out to me, but I ignored it. I didn't know how to move out without being ungrateful.

Two days later, I packed my meager belongings, said my goodbyes and made my way to the Grand Tikal Hotel. Lily and I spent our days playing in the outdoor swimming pool and exploring the underground mall attached to the hotel while I awaited my dad's arrival. A week later, he arrived in the private taxi I had arranged for him. It was wonderful to be together again. I felt more whole, like finding a matching piece of a jigsaw puzzle. Lily's face flashed with recognition when she saw him. She toddled toward him, her arms spread wide as he got down on the floor to greet her, engulfing her in a great big bear hug. I was so overwhelmed with love that I had happy tears running down my face.

Shortly after he came, my new flip phone lit up with Camila's name and number. I hoped she was calling to let me know that she had finally resubmitted our case back into PGN. There was a sense of urgency in her voice. "Kim, get out of that hotel immediately," she said. I didn't understand. A million things went through my head. *Why? What's going on? Is everything all right?*

"It's Karen. She just called. She is coming to Guatemala tomorrow morning and is staying at the Grand Tikal. You've got to get out of there now before she arrives."

I had gone behind Karen's back to work exclusively with Camila, and now I had to get out of there quickly. I made a few calls, packed up my things, and found an inexpensive hotel nearby for the three of us until I could find an apartment in Antigua.

In Antigua, I found an affordable two-bedroom, tastefully furnished apartment on the second level in a gated community within walking distance of the center of town. I had always been friendly and outgoing, but how on earth was I supposed to meet other people when I didn't have a single connection? It was like I was back in ninth grade again when my parents made me transfer schools in the middle of the school year.

Three days after moving to Antigua, I headed to Central Park, with Lily safely buckled into her jogging stroller. I had learned from previous visits that a jogging stroller was the only way to navigate the ancient cobblestone sidewalks and roadways in Antigua. The Central Park was a hub of activity. There were shoeshine boys, tourists, a variety of vendors hawking their wares, as well as Antigüeños sitting or strolling through the park. I figured if I was there long enough, I would meet some other adoptive parents. I sat on one of the wrought-iron benches and let Lily play in one of the small fountains in the park. Nearby, I noticed two fair-skinned women about my age toting Guatemalan infants strapped to their chests. They had just sat down, so I walked over to them and started a conversation, hoping that I did not come across as a total stalker chick.

"Hey, do you live in Antigua?" I felt like it was a cheesy pick-up line, but I was desperate to meet other adoptive moms.

"Yes," the tall, outgoing blonde said, "My name is Carissa, and this is my friend Julie."

Julie shook my hand and gave me a warm smile. We made small talk for a while, then eased into the typical adoptive parent conversation.

"What agency are you using?" I asked.

Carissa rattled off some agency I had never heard of, but Julie said, "Project Oz." My mouth dropped open.

"Project Oz as in Karen at Project Oz?"

"Yes, that Project Oz. I've been fostering little Sebastian here for almost two months. We'll be going home soon. We're just waiting for his birth certificate." I was dumbfounded. How was this possible? Karen had told me numerous times that no one was permitted to foster due to the political climate.

"Do you mind sharing the name of your attorney?"

She rattled off a name I wasn't familiar with.

"And Camila?"

"Never heard of her," she said.

———————————————————

A few days before Christmas, my dad, my husband, my sister and her family arrived at my apartment in Antigua in the private van I had arranged for them. When I heard the brass knocker on the large wooden door to the courtyard, I bounded down the stairs to greet them, with Lily trailing behind. I couldn't believe it. They came. This was real. I hadn't been sure my sister would make the trip since she's afraid of active volcanoes and earthquakes and was very protective of her two small children, both of whom were under four-years-old. But she faced her fears on my behalf. I'd been waiting twenty months—since Lily's referral—for my worlds to meet, and now it was really happening! We were all going to be together for Christmas.

When I saw my niece and nephew, I pulled them into a big bear hug and planted tender kisses all over their heads. I had missed them so much. I'm sure they wanted their Aunt Kimmie to stop, but I couldn't control myself. Lily, now standing nearby with her daddy and Pop-Pop, followed my lead and gave everyone great big hugs, almost knocking over her cousin Aly, who was the same age. Within a few minutes, the kids had warmed up to one another and were fast friends, running up and down the cobblestone street squealing with delight. It was like they had spent the last year and a half growing up together. I was overflowing with happiness.

In addition to the blessing of having our family together at Christmas, my dad brought packages of cards, books, treats, and small gifts for Lily from our friends, our church family, my colleagues, and my school PTA; he even brought a loaner laptop, so I wouldn't feel so cut off from the world. That evening, as I opened each token of love, tears of thankfulness streamed down my cheeks. I often had to pause while reading a card or letter because the flow of emotion was so much. I had never felt so loved or supported as I did at that moment. I did absolutely nothing to deserve any of their kindness, and yet our entire community poured out its love to my family in abundance. It was the most magical Christmas ever, a true expression of God's great love for me.

Chapter 17

In January 2008, the paid leave I had saved up over the last eleven years of employment finally ran out, and Olav had to support us on his drafting salary of less than thirty five thousand dollars a year. With our income cut substantially, I felt extremely vulnerable. How much longer could we sustain two residences? We had planned for only six weeks, and now twelve weeks later, Lily's case was no farther along than it had been in October. *How much longer would this take?* I wondered. I also wondered where we would come up with the ten thousand dollars in fees Project Oz required when our case would exit from PGN. I tried to push these fears out of my head, but they lingered like a houseguest who has stayed too long.

In early February Olav was due to fly to Guatemala. Two weeks before his visit, he told me over the phone that he had some unexpected news he wanted to share with me in person. I tried to pry it out of him, but he insisted he had to share this information in person. In typical Kim fashion, I began to think the worst. Olav had cancer, his mother was sick and dying... my mind went wild with possibilities.

When Olav finally got to my apartment in Guatemala, and after I made him a cup of coffee, we sat down on the sofa together, our knees touching. Like a doctor delivering a bad diagnosis, he said, "I got let go from my job."

I had not expected this at all. "Did they give you a reason?" I asked.

"Kimmie, it was all scripted. They didn't tell me I was fired outright, more like we are letting you go so you can focus on getting your daughter home from Guatemala."

I began to unravel as the truth of the situation sank in. I couldn't sit still. I began to pace in circles in my living room in a feeble attempt to burn off the growing anxiety within me. "Oh my gosh, what are we gonna do? I'm not earning any money right now, and now you're unemployed." All I could think was that we were about to lose everything: our house, our cars, and most important, Lily.

Maybe it was because he had already processed the situation, but Olav remained calm. "Kimmie," he said, gently taking my hands in his. "Please don't catastrophize. I know this is big, but maybe this is the catalyst I needed to start that architectural drafting business I've always dreamt about."

I trusted Olav, but with neither of us having an income and the money from our savings account and home equity loan dwindling, things looked pretty bleak. We still had to pay for living expenses in Guatemala and the fees to complete the adoption should our case ever get through PGN.

Since Olav was no longer employed and he had racked up some frequent flyer miles, I asked him if we could change places for a short time so I could go home and recharge my emotional batteries. I wanted to drive my car, see my friends, walk through the aisles of Target, and throw my toilet paper in the actual toilet (in many developing countries toilet paper cannot be thrown in the toilet because of the poor septic system). In March we decided to change places for two weeks. He was ecstatic about being able to be a full-time daddy while mommy got some much needed respite.

At home, I enjoyed long hot showers and using an actual washer and dryer. Five days after leaving Guatemala, I was folding my laundry in the living room when the HR director from my job called. Diego had always been straightforward, so when the conversation started out, I was already bracing for the worst.

"There's not enough projected enrollment for two full-time PE teachers at your current school for next year. Because you are on leave, we have to give the position to your colleague. If you return from leave, we will reassign you somewhere else in the county."

"Thanks for letting me know." But all I could think of was my job, my students and their families, and my coworkers who were like family to me. They were all gone, just like that. Not to mention that now, no one was earning an income in our household.

"Sure thing, Kim," he said, trying to sound encouraging and upbeat. "I know things have been difficult, so I didn't want you to get hit by any extra unexpected surprises."

After the call ended, I kept playing the conversation over

and over in my head. For a brief moment, I pondered calling him back. *Maybe I could negotiate something. After all, I had seniority in the county.* Then again, even if I did try to negotiate, it would mean returning to work immediately and giving up on Lily or pitting me up against my coworker, whom I highly regarded. It was a no-win situation.

Even before the job losses, doubt had begun to creep in. But now, with the threat of potentially sacrificing everything with no guarantee that Lily would ever come home, I wondered if this adoption was really God's will or my own selfish will. I had been so focused on what I wanted, but what if God had different plans?

In the book of Genesis, the first book in the Bible, God told Abraham to take his only son, Isaac, whom he loved dearly, and sacrifice him as a burnt offering on the mountain. It is completely unfathomable that a loving God would ask His people to sacrifice that which is most valued to them, and yet that is exactly what God asked of Abraham. He was testing Abraham's faithfulness.

I kept this lesson in mind when I returned to Guatemala a week later. One evening after putting Lily to bed, I sat in the blue floral armchair in my living room. Tears filled my eyes as I cried out to God. "Is this what you have called me to? Are we supposed to lay her down at the proverbial altar?" I didn't like it, but God was peeling back my tightly grasped fingers one by one. He wanted me to surrender her, not as an act of defeat but an act of faith—faith in Him and His goodness.

A few days later, before bed, I began bargaining with God. "God if we don't save her, who will?"

His answer was unmistakable, almost audible. He said, "Kim, I am her Savior; you are not."

I fell humbly to my knees, face down on the tile floor with tears streaming down my face. His message was overwhelmingly clear; God didn't need me to rescue Lily. She was His child, not ours. He wanted me to surrender my will completely to His will and unclasp my tightly clenched hands.

I understood, but still I begged, "Can we have the privilege of becoming her parents?"

A few moments later, through my tears, I heard God whisper, "Lily will come home." I didn't know what that meant or how long it would take, but I held onto that promise with all my might as the storm raged on.

With both of us essentially unemployed, Olav was forced to head back to the States to launch his residential architectural drafting business. I realized that I desperately needed to find a way to bring in an income too.

Through the local newspaper, I found two local language schools seeking an English as a Second Language teacher. The first interview was with a stout Guatemalan woman who never stopped frowning, but the second interview seemed promising. The man was English and had been teaching in

Guatemala for twenty years. After the interviews, he gave me the news I'd been hoping for. "I'll give you twenty an hour, for fifteen hours a week. You'll start tomorrow." I was pleased with myself. I might not be making a teaching salary, but it would be more than enough to offset our living expenses in Guatemala.

I called later that night to confirm the details of our arrangement. In his British accent he said, "Twenty dollars!? I don't pay twenty dollars. I pay twenty *quetzales.*" This was about three dollars per hour. Thank goodness I was on the telephone because I was so embarrassed my face turned crimson with shame. I don't know how I thought I could possibly earn a living wage in Guatemala.

I thought I was out of options when a friend from the States who worked as a fifth-grade teacher at my school sent me a job notice for the international school in Guatemala City. They were looking for a physical education teacher for grades six through twelve. The job was perfect. I could earn a real salary, and it was something I really wanted to do.

After the initial interview, the headmaster, a woman in her sixties with a warm smile and a thick Midwestern accent, invited me back for a second interview. She said, "You're our top candidate; we are very interested in you."

Restraining my exuberance, I gave her a firm handshake. "I'm very interested, too!" I said confidently.

The only caveat was the job required a two-year commitment. I had no idea how much longer Lily's adoption would take. It could continue to drag out for many months or even years. Nevertheless, once we finished Lily's paperwork, the plan was to return to the United States; however, a two-year commitment would mean remaining in Guatemala regardless of whether her adoption had been completed.

By mid-April, we had nearly burned through all the money we had from our savings and home equity loan. I had yet to be offered a job, and Olav was doing his best pounding the pavement looking for work, but building clients took time. I was beginning to panic. I wasn't sure if we would have enough money to pay our next mortgage payment, let alone our living expenses.

Just when I thought we were about to go under, I received a phone call from Marilyn, the worship director at our church.

"Kim, I know things have been tough financially for you and Olav." She had an idea for the church to host a music festival fund-raiser on our behalf. I began to cry. Marilyn had no idea how divine her timing was.

"You would do that for us?" I replied, truly humbled at her kindness.

"Of course, we love you guys." The plan was to call it Lilypalooza and have a big music festival, with a chili cook-off, and a silent auction to help raise funds.

When I got off the phone with Marilyn, I thought to myself, *who am I, God, that you are mindful of me?* It was as if God stepped down from heaven and wrapped His giant arms around me.

A few weeks later, I got an interesting job lead. I had heard about an American family who had recently relocated to Guatemala. They were looking for a tutor to help homeschool their kids while they were completing their Guatemalan son's adoption. I was terrified that they might not consider me suitable. After all, I was not a traditional classroom teacher, but Linda, the mother, was a very progressive mom and loved the idea of my kinesthetic approach.

I met with her children a few times, and by word of mouth, my tutoring business in Guatemala took off. Before I knew it, I was getting calls from several families, both American's living in Antigua and wealthy Guatemalan families wanting me to tutor their children. For the first time since Olav lost his job, I was able to help cover some of my rent and living expenses.

Six months had passed since Olav and I had lived together in the same house, and we missed each other. I was growing weary of parenting alone, plus he was missing so much of Lily's growth and development. I didn't want our family to be separated any longer. I had the perfect solution. One evening while Olav was visiting, we sat down on the sofa after putting Lily to bed and he started massaging my shoulders.

I innocently asked, "What do you think about me taking the Physical Education job here in Guatemala?" I had been reluctant to agree to a two-year commitment, but now I was starting to see it as a real opportunity. "We could live off my salary, and you could come to live here with me permanently."

Olav immediately stopped massaging my back, "Are you

out of your mind? If you accept that job, you'll be stuck here another two years. Is that really what you want?"

Clearly, he didn't understand my logic. I didn't want to stay in Guatemala any longer than necessary, but I also didn't want to leave if her adoption wasn't completed by August. By taking the job, I would be ensuring that I wouldn't have to leave her. "Besides," he said, "what am I going to do down here?" Olav's drafting business was just getting off the ground, and he had started doing some work for a wealthy philanthropist. "I am confident I can make a lot more money in the States than I could down here in Guatemala. Plus you don't even have the job yet."

I knew he was right, but I asked him to pray with me, seeking God's direction. I no longer wanted to rely on my limited knowledge, but wanted God to lead me. After much prayer and discussion, we decided that, regardless of whether Lily's adoption had been completed or not, I would return to work in the United States. Even though it seemed counterintuitive to plan my departure before Lily's adoption was possibly completed, I felt strangely at peace with our decision. Although I wouldn't be able to take my old job, Diego had said that they'd find a position for me at a different school.

Preparing to start over again with new students and new colleagues, I was surprised when I got a call from Diego a few weeks later.

"The principal at your old school really wants you back. Student numbers at his school have increased, and he now has the staffing for a four-day-a-week physical education teacher. Would you be interested even though it is only part-time?"

"Yes," I said in amazement. "That would be perfect." If I had to go back to work, this was the ideal scenario. I would still make close to a full salary, resume my benefits, and have a long weekend every week, should I need to commute back to Guatemala to visit Lily.

The day after I recommitted to my job, my phone rang again. This time it was the headmaster from the international school. I imagined her sitting behind her desk, hair tied back in a neat bun, peering through her glasses about to read me the details of the contract. Instead she said, "Thank you for your interest in the American School of Guatemala. We've have decided to give the position to another candidate." I was dumbfounded, as I had always been so confident that the job was mine if I wanted it. How presumptuous of me.

I kept having to remind myself that God was in control, not me.

Chapter 18

)n mid-December, three weeks after moving to Antigua, I was checking my e-mail at my neighbor's apartment when I received a suspicious message from Project Oz. It was from a woman named Amanda Smith, who claimed to be a lawyer who sat on the board of directors for Project Oz. I had heard of Heidi, Dina, and Karen but never Ms. Smith. It read:

> I am sorry to inform you, but after numerous frustrating attempts to provide accurate information to Project Oz clients, the Board of Directors have released Karen from her position as CEO and International Adoption Coordinator. In retaliation, she has emptied the Project Oz bank account and has disappeared with all our clients' financial and adoption records. I will be traveling to Guatemala shortly to meet with Project Oz facilitators and attorneys to see what is needed to complete your cases. In the meantime, please consider hiring a private Guatemalan attorney, such as

Adoption Supervisors to help you navigate the
adoption process.

I sat there in disbelief. A flood of emotions surged through
me. On the one hand, I was overflowing with thankfulness to
God for the privilege of living in Guatemala when this deluge
of information came through. I couldn't even imagine the terror that the other families in the process must have felt when
they received this news. Had I been stateside, I think I would
have needed to be admitted to a psychiatric hospital.

On the other hand, I wondered how on earth would we
ever recoup the money we lost, and how could we come up
with more money to complete the adoption. I didn't have the
answers, and because I was so overwhelmed, I just had to
trust that somehow it would all work out. Thankfully, we had
already hired Fernando at Adoption Supervisors over a year
ago, and I now understood that Camila worked as an independent contractor for several agencies, including Project Oz.
Even though Project Oz had put up a powerful façade, it was
Camila who was the real puppet master. Project Oz simply
held the purse strings. I believed that as long as I stayed on
Camila's good side, our adoption could continue.

———————————■———————————

Shortly after Karen disappeared, Camila called me. "Kim, I
need six hundred bucks," she said urgently.

Just two months earlier, I had gone back to the United
States the previous October and given this woman the near

impossible; I had updated our immigration paperwork, gotten new fingerprints, updated our home study and paid for new medical reports and clearances all costing over fifteen hundred dollars, and now she wanted more money. I guess it shouldn't have been a surprise since with Karen out of the picture Camila's money supply had dried up. It seemed like the extortion was never ending.

"Your lawyer of record, Javier, is leaving for the States in two weeks, and he won't turn over the power of attorney for your case until I pay him the money."

I had caught a whiff of the rumor that Javier might leave the country a few months earlier, so I had been proactive and asked Fernando about possibly utilizing a more reputable attorney. "Why don't you let me choose my own attorney?" I asked Camila. "Fernando knows of several reputable attorneys we can use."

"No, no, we will use my new lawyer Óscar, he gets things done."

Even when I insisted that we use Fernando's attorney, she refused. "Fernando's attorney has said negative things about me. He is not on our side."

I tried to reason with her, but she was adamant. What could I do? She was the only person who had contact with Lily's birth mother, and we needed her consent to complete Lily's adoption. So either I had to come up with six hundred dollars, or I could kiss Lily goodbye forever.

On December 11, 2007, the landscape of Guatemalan adoptions changed forever when the Guatemala Congress passed the Ortega Law, which halted adoptions indefinitely. Words like *Hague Convention, stolen children, political corruption, Central Authority,* and *baby trafficking* began to be thrown around like candy being tossed during a parade. Not being a politically savvy person, I struggled to make sense of it all, but as I began to hear and read stories, I knew things were not good.

One day, I read an article in the *Prensa Libre,* the most widely circulated Spanish newspaper in Guatemala, about a well-known adoption lawyer who had been denounced by PGN for allegedly stealing an eleven-month girl from her Guatemalan birth parents. Could it really be that children were being taken from their parents and put up for adoption?

Another day while sitting with a group of mothers, all in the midst of adoptions, Deb from LA, whom I had met over a year earlier over breakfast at a hotel in Antigua when she was completing the adoption of her first daughter Pilar, told us she was noticing all kinds of red flags which was causing her to reconsider her second daughter's adoption. "I think my daughter's DNA test has been falsified. The official DNA report was dated on a day that Harper was in my custody."

I couldn't even imagine walking away from Lily, and yet here was a woman whom I highly respected who was seriously reconsidering her adoption due to suspicion of fraud. Even the US government had recently added additional DNA testing safeguards to ensure that a child presented at the start of the process—when the mother was also DNA-tested to ensure she was the child's biological parent—was the same child who received a visa at the end.

Up until December 31, 2007, Guatemalan adoptions had been processed with very little government oversight. With the newly passed adoption law, the Guatemalan government under pressure from the United States and its own human rights activists, and NGOs, began its effort to overhaul its adoption system. Any adoptions not completed prior to December 31, 2007, would not be permitted to continue until they were registered with the newly established governmental Central Authority. I wondered if the government would figure out a way to grandfather those of us in the process, or would adoptions be ceased forever? I tried my best not to get worked up about it, but I was so discouraged. It felt like all I did was jump from one obstacle to another. I waited with adoption advocates and two thousand other families in the process to see what would happen. Many people asked us, "How are you holding up?"

I didn't know how to respond, so I turned to journaling. One day I wrote, "We are laid bare; we have no strength of our own. We are running a race that is long and grueling, but quitting, although at times is tempting, is not an option. We constantly question God, asking why He has allowed this to happen? What purpose is it serving?" After all those years of trying to have a child, this was supposed to be the easy way to create a family. I was learning that nothing in adoption was easy.

Finally, in early January 2008, the Guatemalan government decided that all adoption cases in progress could continue if they registered with the Central Authority. The first Central Authority document was a simple one-page document that even Camila, who had proven herself completely worthless when it came to completing paperwork well, could complete and file without any issues. It was essentially foolproof. With Fernando's guidance, Camila got the paperwork in on time. At that moment, I was so incredibly joyful our case could continue.

However, my happiness was short-lived. A few weeks later, a new Guatemalan president was elected, and the new government officials cried foul. All adoption cases had to re-register with a brand-new Central Authority in a new location and with new staff. To make matters worse, the Guatemalan government gave the lawyers and facilitators only three days to register the cases with only five clerks accepting paperwork from 9 a.m. to 3 p.m. It seemed like the new government was trying to cease all adoptions by making it extremely difficult to register cases. Furthermore, unlike the original registration form, the new registration form was a four-page curriculum vitae, which was sure to throw Camila for a loop. It was like walking backward on a treadmill; my calves were screaming out in pain.

February 11 became the only date that mattered. All adoption cases needed to be registered with the Central Authority before February 11, 2008, or it was game over. I couldn't bear the thought of coming this far only to lose it all. For days leading up to the deadline, my mind raced like a car stuck in overdrive. I played various scenarios over and over in my head, the what-ifs constantly ruminating. *What if we don't get registered in time? What if Camila screws up our paperwork? What if our case is rejected?*

I tried desperately to calm myself, keeping myself busy playing tour guide to my visiting friend Debbie, but no matter how hard I tried to be in the moment, I could hear little voices in my head whispering, "Lily's case will never be registered. It's over. Pack it up. Go home."

Camila assured me that everything possible was being done, that her new attorney, Óscar, was handling things. Still, I had my doubts. After all, Camila had lied to me before.

On February 11, during the final hours of the last day that cases could be registered, the shrill ringing of my phone startled me. It was Camila. My hands were trembling so badly I almost dropped the phone. She sounded frenzied, and I knew that my worst fears were coming true.

"Kim, your file has been rejected. Something is wrong with the filing of your new power of attorney."

I began to sweat, my heart raced, and I shook uncontrollably. I had the sensation of being present in my body and yet not present, like I was separated from myself. I told myself this was a bad dream; it wasn't really happening. I heard Camila speaking to me way off in the distance, reassuring me that she would take care of things, but I didn't trust her. I couldn't imagine losing Lily...losing her would be a fate worse than death. I had to do something. I did the only thing I knew to do, I called Fernando. Thankfully, he picked up immediately.

Hearing the calm in his voice on the other end of the line helped a little bit. "I've been checking in with Camila all morning and already knew your case had been rejected. I've been working diligently to fix the mistake. The Central Authority has extended their hours today to make sure all the lawyers and facilitators in line have a chance to submit their documents. I will make sure your case will be submitted by the end of business today."

I had no other choice but to put my faith in Fernando.

At 7:30 in the evening, there was just one hour to go before the extended hours of the Central Authority would cease registrations forever, and I had yet to hear from Camila or Fernando. My friend Debbie had been praying throughout the day and sharing Bible verses, reminding me that God was in control. I told myself, "Calm down. Don't get yourself into a tizzy. There's still one more hour until the Central Authority closes. Remember, Kim. Time is relative in Guatemala, it might be as late as 9:30 or 10 p.m. before you hear from them."

Finally, at 9 p.m. the telephone rang. I jumped up, nearly knocking over the chair. It was Fernando. "Good news, Camila just called. Lily's case was registered. I'll call you tomorrow to follow up."

My knees buckled as I fell into Debbie's embrace, sobbing tears of relief. The stress of the past few days overwhelmed me. She held me and rocked me like a young child, murmuring prayers of thanks to God. I have no idea how they got it done. I can only attribute it to God's extraordinary intervention on my behalf.

After this small victory, however, two months later, it seemed as if we were back where we had started. Camila had still not managed to resubmit our documents to PGN. I called her nearly every day, and I was getting nowhere. Each day she would say, "I'll submit it tomorrow."

With no real income, an ever-increasing debt load, and the constant fear that perhaps this was all for naught, we were getting desperate. I met with Fernando to review our options.

Outside of riding out the storm, both of them were unthinkable: either turn Lily over to the Guatemalan Minor's court, which would ensure she would be placed in a state-run orphanage and unlikely to be matched with us, or leave Lily at Camila's aunt's house for foster care while I went back to the States to work. I couldn't bear either of those options; I had to stick it out.

Several days before Lily's second birthday, an acquaintance suggested we reach out to Mr. B, who had powerful ties to the current regime of the Guatemalan government. My initial thought was Guatemala Mafia, but I am ashamed to admit that by then I didn't care.

Two days later, we arranged to meet Mr. B in the lobby of the Camino Real hotel, one of the most upscale hotels in Guatemala City. Olav and I sat on a blue velveteen sofa in a little sitting area off to the side of the lobby and waited.

The plush sofa felt wonderful against my skin. I sank into the couch, willing my body to relax. Olav sat down beside me and placed a comforting arm around my shoulders. As we waited, we saw well-dressed bellmen with shiny black shoes quickly moving luggage carts through the marble-floored hallways. A few well-to-do adoptive families passed by, as well as some Guatemalan businessmen.

At precisely 9:00 a.m., I saw an imposing Guatemalan man in an expensive suit with a thick head of salt and pepper hair stroll through the lobby. His eyes met mine, and he walked over to introduce himself.

"I'm Mr. B, a family friend of the Curtis family." His English was impeccable. "Let's get down to business. I've got a meeting across town in one hour." He looked at his Cartier watch encrusted with diamonds, and it occurred to me that it probably cost half as much as my house. "My friend tells me you are having some issues with Camila?"

As I detailed the past two years of struggles during our adoption process, he listened impatiently. I wasn't sure whether to talk more quickly or skip over the details. So I tried to focus on the most critical points: Right now, our case has been kicked out of PGN for nearly one year. According to Camila, our case is ready to be resubmitted to PGN, but despite being registered with the new Central Authority, she has yet to resubmit our documents and therefore, our case is essentially stalled.

When I was finished, he leaned back in his chair, as if we had no reason to worry. "I've worked with Camila numerous times before. I have some dirt on her that will make her squirm. We'll make a plan to bring your baby home."

I wondered what he knew about Camila that we didn't. I felt a slight tinge of guilt. Had we gone over to the other side? No, Camila deserved this. Besides, in the end, we were doing this for Lily. We needed to do whatever it took to bring her home. We left the hotel with a renewed bounce in our step.

That weekend, Mr. B picked us up in his shiny black BMW sedan and escorted us to his lawyer's office in Zone 10 of the city. This place was classy even by US standards. It had an over-the-top Ritz Carlton glam element to it with leather studded chairs, plush carpeting, and drippy chandeliers on the ceiling. We were definitely out of our element.

Two attractive secretaries dressed in bright formfitting dresses greeted us with smiles plastered on their faces. They instructed us to sit in the sunken waiting room overlooking the city and offered us a choice of coffee, tea, or water.

A few minutes later, the lawyer came out. He was impeccably dressed in a crisp olive green suit and polished black wingtip shoes. His hair was slicked back a little too perfectly. He shook our hands as his large silver Tiffany ID bracelet peeked out. He reeked of money. In a country where most people made less than a dollar a day, he was an anomaly.

He looked over at Mr. B. "Mr. B and I are good buddies with the director of PGN, Señor Reyes," he said. "We will use our contacts to get your daughter's case out of PGN immediately." All he needed was for us to sign a few papers and—here was the glitch—five thousand dollars.

Olav and I looked over at each other and swallowed hard. It was a lot of money, money we didn't have. Still, I knew my dad thankfully would loan us the money if we decided to go this route. Having finally gotten financially stable prior to pursuing Lily's adoption, I knew that taking on new debt would weigh heavy over my head.

Then there was the more significant issue: was this right? I think Olav and I both had a nagging suspicion this wasn't entirely on the up-and-up, but we were so desperate. I am ashamed to say that I suppressed my doubts. I told myself: it's the only way; we've tried everything else. Nothing has worked. We have to do something.

"We'll sign the papers, but no money until we have the evidence," I said. Being in Guatemala had taught me at least one thing: you never give money to anyone until the job is done.

Surprisingly, they agreed to our terms. Either we were shooting ourselves in the foot, or we were on the path home. Either way, I wasn't going to just sit around doing nothing anymore.

———————————————

A few days after meeting with the new lawyer (whom Olav and I began to call Mr. Fast Track due to his slick persona), we had the opportunity to throw Lily a real second birthday. During my time in Antigua, I had met Pat and Bill, a missionary couple from Southern California. They offered to host a grand celebration for her in the community room attached to the coffee house they ran called Higher Grounds.

With Pat's help, I strung pink and purple streamers from the weight-bearing poles steadying the foundation. Pat set out dozens of pretty pink frosted cupcakes. Green plastic chairs were scattered around the room, while the most awesome pink dinosaur piñata hung from the rafters, just waiting to be hit by the eager children. My dad, my husband, and the entire adoption community living in Antigua gathered around to celebrate Lily's birthday. I wanted to freeze that moment in time, to soak in every sound, sight, and delightful evidence of love and life. I had so many things for which to be thankful.

Out of a sense of obligation, I had invited Camila, Manuel, and their extended family to the party. My fellow adoptive mothers thought I was crazy, especially after hearing the stories of the lies, but I wasn't even sure if they would show. Forty-five minutes into the celebration, Camila and her family arrived carrying a large bouquet of multi-colored pastel balloons. Camila proudly handed me an unwrapped gift. It was a PGN receipt. Both Camila and Fernando had told me the day before that our case had reentered PGN, but I had been reluctant to believe it until I had tangible proof. After nearly a year of waiting, our adoption case was finally back on track. Despite all my bitterness and anger at her for her failing to act so many times on our behalf, I wrapped my arms around her neck, jumping with joy.

"Thank you," I said. "This is the best birthday gift ever!"

———————————————

After being off the PGN train for nearly a year, it was

somewhat exhilarating to be moving again. I was getting periodic reports from both Fernando and Mr. Fast Track, neither of whom knew of the other's involvement. After two weeks in PGN, Fernando called to let us know our case had passed the first reviewer and would be moving on to the second one. I was ecstatic. We had never made it this far in the process. The very same day, Mr. Fast Track called. "Your case is progressing nicely. I should have the director's signature by next Wednesday. I'll take you to PGN, and we'll pick up your paperwork."

While I was beginning to feel cautiously optimistic, I couldn't shake the ominous feeling that signing with Mr. Fast Track was wrong. We hadn't stooped to bribery over a year ago when Karen suggested it, why were we doing it now, and at a much higher price?

That evening before bed I was reading my Bible when a passage jumped out at me: "If anyone builds on this foundation using gold, silver, costly stones, wood, hay, straw, their work will be shown for what it is, because the Day will bring it to light. It will be revealed with fire, and the fire will test the quality of each person's work" (1 Corinthians 3:12-13).

It hit me, like a skillet to the head. What were we thinking? We could lose Lily forever! I wanted out, but it was too late. We had already made our bed; now we had to sleep in it. I was sickened by what a foolish, desperate woman I had become. When was I ever going to put my trust in God and stop relying on myself? I cried out to God, begging for his forgiveness and mercy.

That night, alone in my bed, sleep wouldn't come. The

two young lovers next door were busy having boisterous sex, as if they knew my husband lived over three thousand miles away. I tried to tune out their noise while trying to figure out a way to get out of the situation in which we had put ourselves. After an hour of tossing and turning, I decided to update my blog. I went to my dining room table and turned on my laptop. I decided to check my e-mails first. There in my in-box was a notice from Kevin Kreutner, a well-respected spokesperson and lead writer for Guadadopt, an online Guatemalan adoption community. It stated that the newly elected President of Guatemala decided to clean house at PGN. Except for two lawyers, all the current staff of PGN had been terminated effective earlier today. I couldn't believe it! All of Mr. B's and Mr. Fast Track's connections had been fired from PGN, so unless Mr. Fast Track got the signatures earlier than expected, God saved me from myself. Who am I, God, that you could possibly be mindful of weak-willed and deceitful me? I put my head down on the table and let my tears flow.

The next day, Mr. Fast Track called and left a message. He was no longer smooth-talking. "I got your papers signed before Señor Reyes got fired. You pay me money today," he demanded.

After listening to the threatening tone in his message, I panicked. From what I read online, there was no way he was telling the truth. I went downstairs and knocked on my neighbor Karla's door. She would know what to do.

Karla said, "My people can be very unscrupulous. Don't give him anything until you see your paperwork."

That sounded strangely familiar. I remembered what seemed like many years ago Fernando saying something very similar.

"What if he tries to track me down and find me like a bounty hunter?"

"Don't worry," she said. Gosh, how I hated that saying.

"Don't worry!? How can I not worry?"

"If he got the signature, you pay him the money. No signature, no money. You understand?"

"But what—"

"Trust me. I'm Guatemalan. I know how these people can be."

I was nervous, but I trusted Karla.

The next day Karla and I were hanging out in my living room when Mr. Fast Track came to my apartment demanding his money. "We had a deal," he said. "I got you the signature. You hand over the money." I knew he was lying, but I was terrified. What if he had a knife or a gun? What if he forced me to withdraw money at the ATM?

Karla sprang into action. Unafraid, she came to my side and went head-to-head with him. This girl had grit. "No authentication, no deal. Now get out of here, and leave her alone," she said, before she fired off a few more colorful words in Spanish for good measure.

Mr. Fast Track angrily stormed off, slamming the wooden door behind him. I was so incredibly thankful Karla had my back. I don't know what I would have done without her.

Starting with the firing of Señor Reyes and the PGN staff in late April, adoptions were halted once again. Unlike the Central Authority registration, this time it had a much more foreboding feel to it. The Guatemalan government ordered that all birth mothers who relinquished their children through a private attorney would now have to appear before the PGN authorities. All cases would go before a panel to be scrutinized for signs of corruption and fraud. Lily's birth mother was a poor indigenous woman from the highlands of Guatemala, who, according to the social worker report, could not read or write. Had she been coerced into placing Lily for adoption?

During those days, the police presence in Antigua increased ten-fold, and adoptive parents were strongly warned not to leave our homes with our children. It felt like the government was trying to thwart all foreign adoptions, despite the earlier promise that it would permit all cases that had been registered with the Central Authority to continue.

Even though I had the legal documents to be Lily's foster parent, I hunkered down in my home for three days, heeding the terrifying warnings. I tried my best to carry on as if nothing was different, but I couldn't shake the horrible thoughts in my head. I felt as though I were going to lose Lily; it was just a matter of time.

To make matters worse, reports of children being removed from their foster parents in Guatemala City and Antigua were widespread on the news and Internet. Unannounced raids on local orphanages occurred, with many children being ripped away from everything they had ever known, only to be placed in overfilled state-run *hogares* (orphanages) until the government could investigate. Fellow adoptive foster mothers who helped us celebrated Lily's second birthday two weeks earlier, were now sleeping on dirty floors in lice-infested *hogares*, clinging to their children until the orphanage directors forced them to leave.

I heard of accounts of birth mothers coming out of the shadows and testifying that they were coerced into placing their child up for adoption. Some even claimed their children were stolen from them. I couldn't bear the thought that this could possibly be what happened to Lily and that she could be taken from me forever. I was gripped with fear. Unanswered questions swirled through my head. *What if Lily had been stolen?* Camila wasn't exactly the model of integrity. *What if her birth mother changed her mind?* It had been over two years; maybe her circumstances had changed? *What if the government officials forced Lily's birth mother to recant her consent?* The questions were endless.

Nights were the worst. I still vividly remember one night at 1:30 a.m. I heard a rustling outside my window. Cold terror reached its gangly hands up my chest. I shot up in my bed. *Who could be outside? Is someone stalking us, just waiting to break into our house to snatch my precious daughter from my arms?* I could feel the blood pulsating in my ears as I walked gingerly to the courtyard to check, but there was nothing but the sound of the tree leaves rustling in the wind. My heart was pounding like I just sprinted a 10k. Adrenaline coursed through my veins. I sat down at my kitchen table and opened my laptop. The screen lit up the dark room. With unsteady hands, I typed the words *fear* and *Christian believer* and an online Scripture lesson on fear appeared. As I began reading the lesson to which God had led me, He was speaking to me through the reading and His word. I was reminded that God did not give me a spirit of cowardice or fear, but a spirit of a calm and well-balanced mind (2 Timothy 1:7). The lesson further pointed out that fear was indeed a spirit, and it was not a spirit from God.

I know it sounds otherworldly, but it was in that moment I became acutely aware of the spiritual warfare that I had heard about in my small group Bible studies but had never experienced firsthand. I could literally feel the spirit of fear raging around me. The battle to bring Lily home wasn't just a physical one, but a spiritual one as well. I wasn't sure exactly how to do it, but I needed to stop letting the voices of fear and discouragement always shake me. I needed to put my trust in God and hold on to His promises, even if things seemed impossible.

Two days later, in the early evening, Fernando called to confirm Lily's birth mother interview. I had been so nervous, afraid that Camila wouldn't be able to locate her or that she might change her mind, so I was relieved when Fernando told me the interview was for the next day at noon.

"Kim, get a cab tomorrow morning at 8 a.m. and go to the Project Oz office in Zone 1. Be very careful in Zone 1. Make sure your windows are rolled up all the way and lock your doors. Have the taxi driver escort you into the office as the area is quite dangerous even in daylight."

"Okay," I said obediently.

All morning, I was sick to my stomach, clutching Lily as if I might never see her again. This was the day that would decide Lily's fate. Was her adoption legitimate, or was it part of the dark underworld of corruption, coercion, and human trafficking?

A few hours later, one of my trusted cab drivers picked me up, and we drove into the city. I was thankful that traffic was lighter than usual and that we arrived on time. Not wanting to put Lily or me at risk to be shot, robbed, or abducted in broad daylight, I did exactly as Fernando had told me and kept the windows up and doors locked.

I was all "prayed up" as they say in Christian circles, meaning that I was spiritually prepared for the day, but I had no idea how the day would unfold. Upon arriving in the taxi, I was greeted at the ground level by Camila's brother Juan. The multistoried building was large and imposing. The windows were covered in bars and the off-white paint on the walls was peeling everywhere.

At the entrance of the Project Oz office, I was greeted by

Camila. "I have spoken with Lily's birth mom, and she remains committed to the plan of adoption." I believe this was intended to calm me down, but my nerves were through the roof. Everything was riding on this interview.

Camila gently took my arm and turned me around to introduce me to Lily's birth mother. "Kim, this is Lilian, Lily's birth mother. Lilian, this is Kim Gjerde, the American woman who is adopting Lily."

Lilian was dressed in a traditional *corte* (skirt) with blue and white vertical stripes, held up with a woven floral embroidered belt with a white floral shirt that appeared to be a cross between a traditional *hupil* (a traditional square cut blouse with special embroidery) and a hand- embroidered eyelet top. Noticeably several months pregnant, her face and limbs were swollen. She resembled a much fuller version of the photograph we had received two years earlier with Lily sitting in her lap for the original DNA testing.

Lilian shook my hand limply, "*Con mucho gusto,*" she said, her eyes not making contact with mine. I wondered what she was thinking. Was she as unnerved as I was? Finally, after a few uncomfortable moments, she looked up at Lily with tearful recognition. "*Mi Rosmery,*" she said. (Rosmery was Lily's given middle name.) Lilian reached for her daughter with her two swollen arms and gently pulled Lily into her lap. For a brief minute Lily looked at me with mild alarm, but I gave her a reassuring smile, and Lily, who had rarely known a stranger, soon became mesmerized by her first mom's blouse and began fingering the brightly colored embroidered flowers that stood out.

Unsure if I would ever get this opportunity again, I wanted to learn as much as possible about this beautiful woman sitting before me. "I really like your blouse. Does it have any special significance?" I knew that many indigenous women wore special blouses to signify what town or province they were from.

She seemed to visibly relax and made eye contact with me for the first time. "Yes, it's from my village in Santa Catarina Pinula."

"It's very beautiful," I said, making a mental note to try to find a similar one for Lily.

Lily, never one to sit still for long, began to break out in her favorite song, singing "*Estrellita, ¿dónde estás? Queiro verte cintilar...*" ("Twinkle Twinkle Little Star" in Spanish), while dancing on her birth mother's lap. I laughed in delight and even Lilian cracked a tight-lipped smile.

"Lily really loves to sing and dance," I said. "Every time Lily walks down the street in Antigua, if music is coming from a nearby tienda or car, she will stop, shake her little body and lip-sync to the song, as if she knows all the words." Her birth mom stifled a genuine laugh. She seemed pleased to hear this.

"I really like to sing too," she said meekly, as if having a hobby of her own was forbidden. "I like to sing Christian songs."

"That's wonderful," I replied. "I will make sure to tell Lily when she is older that her mama liked to sing just like her."

Having reconciled with my biological father as an adult, I knew this information could be helpful for Lily in the future. Growing up, I had always identified with my mother because she was the one who was around. I thought I looked like her, sounded like her, and had many of the same idiosyncrasies as her. However, when I reconnected with my biological father as an adult, it was like looking in a mirror. My eyes were his eyes. My mannerisms were his mannerisms. My wanderlust was his wanderlust. In him, I saw pieces of my identity that I didn't even know were missing, and by learning those things, I felt more whole. Aware that Lily had no voice regarding her adoption, the least I could do was give her as many pieces of her biological family as I possibly could.

As we continued to wait for our lawyer, Óscar, to arrive, Lilian seemed to warm up to me as we both playfully interacted with Lily. I desperately wanted to make connections with her, even if our backgrounds and experiences had been very different. Feeling self-conscious and aware that she still had the right to change her mind at any time, I also wanted her to think well of me and to feel secure that I would raise Lily right by her.

I continued to ask her questions, eager to learn as much about her as I could. Did she have any favorite foods? Did she speak *Quiché*, a native Mayan language? What could she tell me about Lily's birth father? What did she think of Lily trying to find her when she was older? Had she been an American birth mother, I may not have asked the more invasive questions, but here in Guatemala, I knew this might be my only chance.

At that moment, despite my anxiety leading up to this day, I sensed that this opportunity was unique. Unlike the majority of the other two thousand foreign adoptive parents still in the pipeline, I was being given this great privilege of connecting with Lily's story of origin. Up until now, Lilian had been just a nameless face on a piece of paper. It was easy to detach from her experience. But now in her presence, I was incredibly humbled by her sacrificial gift of love. I was receiving the truest form of love. She was giving up a part of herself, flesh of her flesh, so that her child could hopefully have a better future than the one she could offer.

An hour later, Camila motioned for me to follow her down a narrow hallway, which connected to a small, dimly lit room. It had one small, dirty window overlooking an empty parking lot. Camila asked me to take a seat across from her desk. I'm not the most organized person, but I couldn't get over the sheer disarray of her office. It looked like she had left the window open and a strong wind had come through. I stepped over stacked books and papers to sit in the green plastic chair across from her desk. I couldn't believe she could process any adoptions at all with the stacks of papers piled high with random documents scattered everywhere. No wonder our adoption paperwork had been such a nightmare.

She picked up a legal-size folder from underneath some

papers with our name on it and began speaking in that serious tone which usually meant she needed something from me. "Your new lawyer, Óscar, said he won't go to the interview with us unless you pay him fifty-five hundred *quetzales.*" This amounted to over 725 dollars.

Fernando had told me I had to pay Óscar two thousand, not fifty-five hundred. It seemed like the extortion would never end.

I called Fernando and he picked up immediately. "Camila is telling me that Óscar won't go to the interview unless I pay him fifty-five hundred *quetzales.*"

Fernando, an expert at this game said, "Kim, pay him what we discussed and see what happens." I was afraid he would refuse to go to the interview, but I trusted Fernando.

Then I walked back into the windowless room with Lily's second foster mother and birth mother and waited for our lawyer to show up so we could go to PGN.

After several hours, in sauntered Óscar. I was expecting a lawyer like Fernando, well-kempt and smartly dressed in a suit and tie, but this guy looked like he belonged on the Las Vegas strip in the 1970s. He was wearing a brown plaid collared buttoned-down shirt. It was unbuttoned down to his chest and tuffs of black hair were peeking out, as though he were channeling his inner Tom Selleck. His khaki pants were rumpled with the whites of the pockets peeking out. His brown dress shoes were scuffed up, his hair was matted to his head, and his eyes were bloodshot, probably from too much alcohol. *This is the guy who is going to represent us in these high-stakes interviews!? We are doomed,* I thought.

He gave me a weak handshake and then asked for the money. I heard Fernando's reassuring voice in the back of my head. "Don't worry, Óscar has gone through fifteen interviews and hasn't had a single issue. Everything will be fine." I wanted to believe him, but I was not so sure.

I gave Óscar the two thousand *quetzales.* He counted it, rolled it up, and placed it in his front pocket. Fernando had been right; Camila had just been trying to extort more money out of me.

We arrived at PGN by 1:20 p.m. From everything I had read about PGN, I had created this huge monster in my head. The actual PGN building, however, looked like any other un-assuming office building built in the 1970s. The back entrance had a handicap accessible ramp (very unusual in Guatemala) with the letters *P, G,* and *N* in the form of a topiary surround-ed by a flower garden to welcome visitors. The inside looked like a dated college hallway with classrooms only on a much larger scale. We went downstairs to where the interviews were taking place.

As we waited to be called, Lilian and I took Lily to the bathroom to freshen up for the interview. Lily needed her hands and face cleaned as well as her diaper changed. As Lil-ian lay Lily down on the bathroom tile trying to change her diaper, Lily whined and whimpered like a puppy. Her birth mother was forceful and threatened to give her the belt and pinned her down. I winced, but I didn't interfere. According to the social worker report, Lilian was the only girl amongst seven brothers, and her mother died when she was a teen. I was sure her life had not been easy. As a "pampered American princess," I was in no place to judge her parenting style. Plus, Lily was still legally her daughter, and she had the right to change her mind any time prior to the completion of the adoption.

When we returned to the waiting area, a woman dressed in an all-black suit standing behind a large podium called, "*El Caso de Lilian Cajas Ramírez.*"

We headed toward the counter. Sitting in the lobby waiting area with Camila beside me, I began my silent prayers.

They appeared to be presenting their identification cards called *cédulas* to the guard when suddenly the discussion grew louder and heated. Óscar was trying to negotiate something with the suited inspector. Once again, my mind began to reel with possible scenarios. *What was the problem? Were we too late for the interview?* After a few moments, they turned around, a look of defeat on their faces.

Vilma, Lily's second foster mother, explained to me that she didn't have her *cédula* with her. Apparently, it was stolen last week, and she hadn't had a chance to get a new one yet. The only identification she had was a copy of her *cédula* in the foster mother papers. That was not sufficient.

There would be no birth mother interview today. I had a difficult time understanding everyone's lack of foresight and planning. Óscar and Camila would have had to have known that authentic identification was needed. After all, this was a legal proceeding.

————————————————■————————————————

Three days later Fernando called to let me know that our birth mother interview had been rescheduled for 10 a.m. the next day. "Kim," he added urgently, "Camila said you asked the birth mother a lot of questions. Please don't do that tomorrow."

I didn't say anything in response, but I wondered why not. I had just wanted to get to know her. *Were they worried that I would find out something terrible?* But Fernando had never steered me wrong before, so I knew to heed his advice.

At 10 a.m. the next morning, everyone had gathered again at Camila's office with the exception of Óscar. I made small talk with Lilian and enjoyed watching her interact with Lily, but I heeded Fernando's advice and remained quiet about personal matters. As time passed, I began pacing the small room as we waited. Both Camila and I tried calling Óscar on his cell phone multiple times with no success. *Where was he? Why wasn't he answering his phone?* In my growing agitation, I glanced at the clock frequently, a constant reminder that the lawyer was late. It seemed like this appointment wasn't going to happen either.

Finally, at 1:30 p.m. Óscar strolled in, completely unfazed that we had been waiting for him for three and a half hours. The teacher in me wanted to reprimand him for keeping us waiting for so long, but I needed to stay in his good graces. I

had really hoped he would present himself more professionally today, but like before, his clothing was rumpled, and his
eyes were still bloodshot. We crammed ourselves into Juan's
red Datsun and headed off to the PGN office. Without the usual traffic, we arrived at 2 p.m., and PGN was swarming with
people. Óscar approached the front desk, inquiring about pro-
curing our interview for the day, even though we were very
late.

I overheard the PGN official say, "Sorry no more interviews available today."

What a three-ring circus this was becoming. It was start-
ing to get ridiculous. First, we missed our interview because
of a missing ID card. Now our lawyer showed up over three
hours late.

As we were leaving the building, we heard the desperate
cry of a young woman. She was running towards Lily shouting, "*Mi hija, mi hija*" (my daughter, my daughter).

She was stopped by the guards. Camila took me firmly by
the elbow as we kept walking forward.

By the time I got home, I was a disaster. I put Lily down
for a much-needed nap and began walking around my apartment tidying up every tiny thing to keep my fears at bay. *Who
was that woman at PGN? What made her think Lily was her
daughter? That couldn't possibly be true, could it?*

To calm myself, I hopped into the shower. Due to my
wimpiness at not being able to tolerate cold showers, the
landlord had installed an electric showerhead. It was called a
"widow maker" because the heating element was attached to

the showerhead with electrical wires sticking out dangerously close to the water.

With a small stream of lukewarm water pelting my skin, I began to unwind. As I got out of the shower and wrapped towels around my body and hair, I heard the familiar ring of my cell phone.

"Everything has been cleared up," Camila said confidently on the other end. "We have a new interview appointment for next week." She explained that, according to the PGN officials, some women, who had been pressured by family members or lawyers to give up their child for money, were staying at PGN each day desperately looking for their stolen children. Apparently, the woman who had run up to Lily had been forced by her husband to give up her child for money. She had spent her days camped out at PGN during the interviews running up to any child who appeared to be the age of her missing little girl.

After I got off the phone with Camila, I ran back into the bathroom and vomited. I couldn't even imagine what kind of threats had been made against that poor woman. To think she was trying to break free and regain control of her life by finding her daughter. It was beyond my comprehension. And while I was fairly confident that Lilian was indeed Lily's mother, it was distressing to think that many parents could be adopting a child who was stolen from their birth mother.

The following week, we arrived at PGN by midmorning. By then, I had chewed up the entire inside of my mouth, and my jaw was sore from clenching my teeth for days on end. *I hope all the clowns involved in this circus show up on time and do their job!*

As we were waiting inside the building for Óscar to arrive, I shifted in my seat, tapped my foot quickly on the linoleum floor, and pressed the ends of my hair into my mouth, a nervous habit of mine.

Lily's birth mother remained outside. I swore I could see tears filling her eyes. I could only imagine the gut-wrenching pain she must have been going through, having to see her daughter three times while waiting to confirm a decision she made over two years ago. Of course, with each time, I was terrified that Lilian might have a change of heart and decide to keep Lily.

Once again, Óscar strolled in an hour and a half late. The PGN official came to the door, "*El Caso de Lilian Cajas Ramírez, por favor.*"

This was it. The moment of truth. Was Lily's adoption legitimate? Would there be red flags? Would it be permitted to continue? I paced and prayed as I waited. After what seemed like half an hour, Lily and the crew exited the large metal door. There was a heavy pause. I stood quietly, awaiting my fate. Vilma took my elbow and started walking with me. She broke into an easy smile as if she knew the agony I had been experiencing and whispered, "Kim, it went well. I believe they will let the adoption continue." She pressed me into her chest and hugged me tightly partly in celebration and partly as if her body could prevent me from falling apart right then and there.

After the interview, Camila took me back to her office and asked to speak with me alone in her back room. "Kim, I need two thousand *quetzales* (approximately $250) to pay for the transportation costs for Lilian and the baby finder."

I was stunned. First, with the exception of paying the lawyer Óscar during our first interview attempt, neither Fernando nor Camila had mentioned paying anyone for anything in regards to this interview, and now she was asking for "transportation costs." I had been in Guatemala long enough to know that bus fare wasn't that much and even a private taxi ride of about an hour would be less than five hundred *quetzales*. I had a feeling this wasn't about transportation costs at all. I had always assumed that Camila was the connection to Lily's birth mother, as Fernando had told me so many times, but apparently, she had used a baby finder, called *buscadoras* or *jaladoras*, who recruited pregnant women to relinquish their babies.

I began to question everything I had been told. Had Lilian really placed Lily for adoption voluntarily because her boyfriend was pressuring her to abort, or was this a business deal with Lilian's birth mother possibly getting something in return from the *buscadora*? I didn't know the answer, and I didn't know what to do. I tried to call Fernando's office but got no response. I tried his partner Jaime. Again no response. Maybe a better woman would have walked away, but I was so in love with Lily. I would have done anything at this point to bring her home. I had to pay up or risk losing Lily.

Not carrying that type of cash on me, Camila called in her

brother Juan (who appeared out of nowhere) to escort me to the nearest ATM on the ground floor of the building. I withdrew two thousand *quetzales*, stuffed the cash in my bra, and went back upstairs. Upon my return, Camila and the *buscadora* were waiting for me in Camila's office. I decided that if I had to pay, I was going to make sure that Lilian received her "transportation costs" paid to her directly. I handed one thousand *quetzales* to the baby finder and the other thousand to Lilian. I looked at Camila and said, "This should take care of the transportation costs." I just hoped they wouldn't rob Lilian after I left. I called my cab driver to come pick up Lily and me. We were so ready to go back home.

I left Camila's office that day feeling like the dirtiest person in the world. This was exactly one of the reasons adoptions were being shut down, and I had an unexpected front-row seat. And yet despite it all, later that day, Fernando called and shared the news I had been hoping and praying for. "The PGN officials officially released a declaration that Lily's adoption is indeed legitimate and will be permitted to continue."

"Thank you," I said in an exhausted daze before hanging up the telephone. While I was incredibly thankful to hear this news, I still wasn't sure it was real. I kept replaying the news over and over in my head in hopes of letting the victory of the situation sink in.

Chapter 19

By now, I had lived in Guatemala for ten months and had made friends with many people. Sonia and Antonio were a married indigenous Guatemalan couple with an infant girl named Cessy. They were live-in housekeepers for a well-to-do Guatemalan family in my neighborhood. While many Guatemalans saw me as Mrs. Moneybags, Antonio and Sonia were genuine friends. When I wanted to purchase a bicycle to get around to my tutoring clients, Antonio took me to his hometown in San Miguel Dueñas and helped me bring a bike back after he negotiated a good deal on my behalf. If I needed something fixed in my apartment, Antonio would volunteer to help me with no qualms or expectations. When Cessy turned one year old, they let me throw her a little birthday party complete with cake and balloons.

Some days we would just hang out on the stoop to the front entrance of their servant's quarters (a small bedroom where the three of them lived humbly) and just talk and laugh. It was one of my favorite ways to pass the time.

Six days after our case had reentered PGN, while I was hanging outside with Antonio and his family, Lily darted into the long narrow entrance hallway past the housekeepers' quarters and turned right into the main house, directly into the formal dining room. Instantly, I bolted after her, knowing what kind of damage the two-and-half-year-old tornado could cause in this fancy house. I was mortified when I looked up and saw the homeowners, Sofía and Jimmy, sitting in the formal dining room with guests. I had no idea anyone would be home, and I was so embarrassed; my cheeks flushed.

"I'm so sorry," I said, trying not to meet their eyes as I caught Lily in my arms and redirected her out of the house. It was as embarrassing as the time Lily ran up front during a Guatemalan friend's daughter's *Quinceañera* Mass (a special religious celebration for girls turning fifteen). She wanted to be with my friend's daughter as she was taking communion. I had been one of only three *gringa* women in the entire Mass, and I had had to run up to the front to bring Lily back!

The next day, Antonio stopped by my place. He said, "After you left, Sofía and Jimmy asked why you were still here in Guatemala. I explained the situation to them, and they would like to talk with you at 3 p.m. tomorrow. They think they can help you." I didn't know what to expect, but I was cautiously hopeful.

The next afternoon, with Lily in tow, I met with Sofía and Jimmy, along with their daughter Ana, who was a lawyer, on their beautiful veranda filled with brightly colored flowering plants.

Jimmy began, "Kim, Antonio tells me you have been trying to adopt this little girl Lily for quite some time."

"Yes, sir," I said politely, as I outlined what the last two and a half years had been like. "We've been visiting Guatemala off and on for nearly two years, and I've spent the last ten months living here." I told them how our adoption agency had gone out of business, leaving us to fend for ourselves. And I explained about how they had been scamming us for money at every turn. "Seven days ago, our case was finally resubmitted to PGN after being kicked out numerous times, and now we are just waiting to see if it will be approved or kicked out again."

Jimmy, a retired attorney, was good friends with the current PGN director Señor Castillo and his wife. "My daughter Ana and I will go and speak to them on your behalf." I was incredibly humbled. These people had just met me, and yet they were willing to go before the head of PGN and intercede for me.

The next evening Jimmy called me. "Señor Castillo has reviewed your paperwork, and it has been signed. It will be ready for pick up tomorrow at 10 a.m." Since he had spoken to me in Spanish, I couldn't believe my ears. I thought for sure I had misunderstood.

The next day Ana took me to PGN. We walked right up to the office of the head of PGN, and his secretary instructed us to simply knock on his door. I couldn't believe this was actually happening. For the past two and a half years, I had struggled to complete Lily's adoption, and now I was about to knock on the door of the man whose signature determined the fate of Lily and my future.

We knocked one time. Then the booming voice behind the door said, "Come in."

As we entered the room, Señor Castillo rose from behind his large wooden desk, revealing his short and portly stature. I'd always imagined the head of PGN to be like the Great and Powerful Wizard of Oz hologram, commandeering and menacing, but Señor Castillo wasn't like that at all; he greeted us with a warm smile. Dressed in a well-tailored black suit with a red power tie, he warmly shook our hands and motioned for Ana and me to have a seat. He and Ana chatted amicably as if he had known her since she was a young girl. I did my best to look relaxed and casual, but under my cool façade, I thought I was going to come out of my skin. For the past two years, I had thought of PGN as this huge government entity just waiting to squash me, and here I was actually sitting in the office of the head honcho of PGN to receive my signed file as if it was nothing.

Finally, after a few moments of small talk, he looked at me through his wire-rimmed glasses, directly in the eyes. "I have heard what you have been through. Thank you for not giving up on your daughter. She's a very lucky girl." He handed me my file showing me that all the required signatures were in order.

I could feel the tears pooling behind my eyes, but I held them back. I wanted to leap over his desk and throw my arms around his neck and scream, "Thank you so much. I am the lucky one," but as kind as he had been, hugging didn't seem appropriate. Instead, as Ana and I stood up to leave, I looked straight into his eyes, hoping to convey the depth of my gratitude, shook his hand firmly, and said, "Thank you so much." I walked outside with Ana before anyone could call us back, saying it was all a big mistake.

I practically skipped to Ana's car, feeling as if the weight of the world had been lifted off my shoulders. I couldn't wait to get back to my place, so I could kiss Lily on the head and tell her she was ours forever and to video chat with Olav and scream, "Lily's adoption has been approved!" Olav was thrilled and incredibly thankful he already had plans to come to Guatemala in a few weeks.

I had been waiting for this moment for so long, and I knew beyond a shadow of a doubt that this was only something God could have orchestrated.

I called Fernando and Camila and told them I had my signed file. No one believed me.

"But how?" Fernando stammered on the phone.

"That's impossible," Camila said.

I just smiled to myself as I thought, *Nothing is impossible with God.*

On August 14, two and a half weeks after her case exited from PGN, Lily's birthmother signed off her final consent on the adoption, and even though we still a had a few logistical steps to complete before we could leave the country with Lily, she was officially declared our daughter by the Guatemalan government. Five days later, Olav flew to Guatemala to stay with Lily while I flew home to the United States to begin my school year. Even though my heart ached at having to leave without her, I knew the next time I traveled to Guatemala, she would be able to come home with us. I prayed that God would make a way so that I wouldn't have to wait too much longer.

One week, two weeks, and then three weeks passed. At long last, I finally got the e-mail from the US Embassy that we had been given a date for our visa interview, which was the very last step before we could take Lily home. I had been so nervous about this day, worried that another Project Oz client who used Camila might have blown the whistle on her and made Lily's exit visa impossible, since it was highly probable Camila would be flagged. But God, in His infinite power, allowed our case to be presented at the US Embassy before this happened. I immediately booked my plane ticket and on September 19, 2008, exactly one month from the time I left them, I returned to Guatemala to join Olav and bring her home.

On Monday, September 22, 2008, Olav and I awoke before sunrise, dressed Lily in her U.S.A. T-shirt given to her by my sister Lisa, and headed to Guatemala City. We stood in line outside the embassy with at least one hundred other eager people waiting to be admitted. I really wished we had someone with us to guide us through this final process like all the other adoptive parents in line. They were accompanied by their adoption agency representative, lawyer, or facilitator, but I had to make do.

Once inside the embassy, we were directed to the American Consulate side where we checked in and received the number twenty, the last number for the day. I was so excited to be there, I didn't even care that we were last and would likely have to wait several hours. I actually relaxed as I made myself comfortable, as comfortable as one can get in one of the molded black plastic chairs bolted to the ground.

As I surveyed the room, all the waiting children were less than one year old. A few were crawling and pulling themselves up on chairs, banging their bottles around, but the majority of them were still tiny infants in their proud parent's arms. Lily, of course, was working the room, charming everyone with her outgoing personality.

To pass the time, I made small talk with some of the other waiting families and read the unspoken question on their minds: "Why is your little girl so much older?" But of course, no one dared to ask. For the first time, I wasn't bitter or jealous of the other families in the room because they were bringing their children home at such young ages, but I was filled with an overwhelming sense of gratitude for my experience.

After two and a half hours of waiting, the room was empty and our number was finally called. We walked toward a small wood-paneled door with a gold and black number 10 sticker that looked like the entrance to a tiny linen closet. We walked into the small room with Lily and closed the door. Inside was a thin stern-looking man with black-rimmed glasses. He sat behind a small desk and proceeded to ask me some questions. There were questions about Lily's birthdate, where was she born, and where would she be living in the United States, and then he said the magic words: "Come back tomorrow to pick up your visa."

Olav gave my hand a tender squeeze, and we looked over at one another and smiled. The embassy agent cracked an elusive smile and said, "Congratulations!"

"Thank you," we replied, shaking his hand before we were on our way.

That evening as Olav, Lily, and I lay in bed together, I wanted to savor the richness of this moment. We were nearly finished! God had done the impossible! Tomorrow we would pick up our visa, and we would really be going home together forever to the United States.

The next day, after we picked up our visa, we boarded a plane to Baltimore by way of Houston, Texas. The immigration officials in Houston took us into a side room to evaluate our paperwork. They smiled brightly as they stamped Lily's paperwork, officially confirming she was a US citizen—probably the most rewarding part of their job.

After a few more hours of travel, we finally landed in Baltimore. It was 11 p.m. We had been traveling since noon Guatemalan time, and I couldn't wait to walk off the plane together. As we headed toward the terminal exit gate, Olav hoisted Lily up onto his shoulders, galloping like a horsey as I pushed her empty stroller. Our friends and family came into view. I saw my sister holding a Welcome Home Lily sign. I let the happy tears stream down my face. This was the moment I had dreamed about for the past two and a half years. As we exited the terminal, everyone began to clap and cheer. Shouts of "Lily!" and "You're here" and "You made it" echoed through the nearly vacant airport terminal.

I couldn't stop smiling as my eyes scanned all the special people who had come out to welcome us home despite the late hour. Our friends waved at Lily, welcoming her home. Lily waved back happily like a Hollywood celebrity. My dad stood nearby, holding a large bouquet of colorful balloons, patiently waiting for his turn to greet Lily. When Lily noticed him and the balloons, her face lit up in a huge grin as she exclaimed "Pop-Pop! *Globos* (balloons)!" Olav took her down off his shoulders, placed her down on the ground, and she ran toward my dad. She threw her arms around him as he handed her the balloons. It was everything I had ever imagined and more. My heart was so full of love and gratitude. We were finally where we belonged. We were home.

Epilogue

After our arrival home in 2008, a class-action Racketeer In-fluenced and Corrupt Organizations (RICO) lawsuit was filed against Karen at Project Oz in federal court. Ultimately no one received any funds, apology, or acknowledgement of her ways. Apparently Karen is now a practicing nurse in Southern Maryland.

A year later, I e-mailed the acquaintance who recommended Mr. B and his fast-track lawyer, hoping to hear that they too made it home. I learned that the Guatemalan Mafia kidnapped Mr. Fast Track. He was later freed but hospitalized. Mr. B was brutally murdered, and the case remains unsolved. That family's little boy never came home. I am so thankful that God saved me from myself. That very well could have been us as well.

As Lily got older, we thought how wonderful it would be to give her a younger sibling. Thankfully, in Maryland, we only had to "foster" Ashton for thirty days, before he legally became our son in 2011. Furthermore, the legal fees to adopt Ashton were a tiny fraction of the nearly $100,000 it cost to complete Lily's adoption. Once again, I thought, *who am I God, that you are mindful of me?*

In 2015, when Lily was nine years old, I took her back to Guatemala for the first time since we had left. Unlike ten years earlier, when Guatemala was swarming with adoptive parents and children, we rarely saw another family like ours, since foreign adoptions officially closed in April 2008. Nevertheless, she enjoyed going back and being immersed in her native language and culture as we visited many of the friends we had made.

We visited several orphanages, where we played with the children and rocked babies. We got to meet and spend time with our sponsored Compassion International child, who is only one year older than Lily. Despite the language barrier, they were the best of buddies, holding hands all afternoon as we explored the children's museum in Guatemala City. That Good Friday, after spending the afternoon in Antigua enjoying the elaborate religious processions and floral carpets, Lily salvaged some of the flowers and pine needles from the trampled floral carpets and brought them back to the house where we were staying. A few hours later, I heard, "Mommy come out and see my *alfombra* (carpet)." I was tickled to see her embracing the Easter traditions of her native land as if it was the most natural thing in the world.

We returned to Guatemala again in 2018. Olav and our youngest son Ashton came this time. We enjoyed a trip to the nearby town of San Antonio Aguas Calientes, where we learned about another child sponsorship program called *Niños con Bendición* and were taught some Guatemalan folk dances by the children there. No doubt, these trips have had an impact on Lily as we have had many opportunities to see both the beauty and the brokenness in her home country.

Lily, now thirteen, bounds into my bedroom prior to bedtime, her teal owl cell phone in hand. She always seems to get talkative after 9 p.m. "*¿Le gusta esta canción, Mamá?*" She says, meaning, Do you like this song, Mom?

"Yeah, who's singing it?" I ask, delighted that she has finally embraced her Spanish. Especially after telling me at age four, when she started preschool, that she didn't want to speak Spanish anymore, because no one else did.

"Shawn Mendes," she says. "It's called 'Treat You Better.' "

"It's got a great beat," I say as she snuggles up against me, pressing her head into my chest. So often I take these moments for granted, but this evening I want to be mindful of this moment, because I am unsure of how much longer she will do this. For now, this is what God has given me, and it is more than enough.

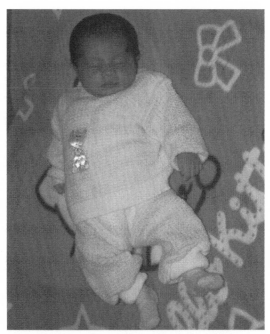

Lily's referral photograph, April 2006

Meeting Lily, August 2006

Home, September 24, 2008

The Gjerde family

Acknowledgements

$\mathcal{F}$ or the past ten years, I have wanted to write Lily's story, but I never felt I was skilled enough. However, I lost a dear friend to cancer in 2017. For me, it was a wake-up call. If you have a dream, you need to do it now, before your life passes you by. Immediately, I signed up for several writing classes online and began to write. As I became more serious, I hired a professional memoir writing coach, Wendy Dale, to help make my goal a reality. Wendy spent many hours reading my manuscript, instructing me, and giving me constructive feedback. Without her guidance, this book would still be in rough draft format. Thank you, Wendy, for everything; it was a privilege to work with you.

In addition to Wendy, there are many others who helped make this book a reality. A big shout out to my early readers Heather Dodson, Val and Sarah Monroe, and Leslie Payne for being sounding boards and providing constructive feedback. For my copy editor, Geoffrey Stone, who took my final manuscript and made it stronger. To my proofreaders, Jessica O'Dwyer, Val Monroe, and Bridget Bergwall, who checked my final manuscript prior to publication and polished it to perfection. To my graphic designer and typesetter, Roseanna White, who had the patience of a saint. Thank you for making my book beautiful. A special thank you to artists Rebecca Giro and Laura Bugash for helping me get the subtitle just right. Also, thank you to my dear friends Allison Benson and Emily Rodgers, for helping me brainstorm suitable subtitles. To my friends, Katie and Dan Rinkes, thank you for photographing your daughter and allowing me to feature her on the front cover of the book. And to make-up artist Jamie Fogle and photographer Diana Boumel, thank you for making me look and feel beautiful in my author photograph.

Lily's adoption never would have been possible had it not been for Lily's birthmother's sacrificial gift of love. The beauty and tragedy of her sacrifice is never lost on me. I hope Lily and I make her proud. Furthermore, her adoption could not have been completed without the financial, emotional, and spiritual support of an overwhelming number of people. Never in my life had I been in a position where people poured out their love on us with no expectation that we could ever repay them for their kindness. Thank you to so many, including, but definitely not limited to; my sister- and brother-in-law; my dad; the Cagle family; the Clarksville Elementary school staff, students and PTA; our friends; and the entire congregation of Monocacy Valley Church. Thank you for being "God with skin on."

I also don't want to forget my dear friends and family members who came to Guatemala to visit me and helped make a difficult situation more bearable. Thank you to Bobbie

Rosnik, Elaine Goebel, Eric Bugash, Collette Julian, Debbie Gravatt, Sharon Gravatt, Ginger Bugash, the O'Masta's, and my dad for leaving your comfort zones and spending time with me. I cherished our time together.

During my time in Guatemala, I had the privilege of meeting some amazing people. Thank you to my neighbors and native Guatemalan friends Karla Aroche, Sonia Matías Poron, and Antonio Chuy, for looking out for me. I don't know where I would have been without you! A heartfelt thank you to all the individuals who helped free Lily and me from the bureaucracy we were stuck in. Thank you for having faith in me. To my fellow adoptive mama's whom I met while living in Guatemala: thank you for being my friends; it was a pleasure to journey beside you. To Pat and Bill Mossman, the YWAM staff at Higher Grounds Coffee House in Antigua, thank you for being a safe place and my sanity in the storm. I love you! Thank you, *Iglesia del Camino*, for opening your doors to me and providing an anchor in the stormy seas. To my wonderful *niñeras* Yolanda and Elaina, who loved Lily like their own and cared for her so I could work. I am humbled and inspired by your work ethic.

God, thank you for teaching me so many valuable lessons during Lily's adoption and for allowing me to parent Lily. I am forever changed by the experience. I hope you are pleased with how we are raising her. I am also incredibly thankful for the gift of Ashton. I remember when you told me, "You will have a baby," and I thought for sure that meant I would physically have a child. Never could I have imagined the awesome little boy you would bless us with through a surprise adoption a few years later. I love and adore him. Last, I want to thank Olav, my husband of over 19 years, for supporting my dream and for always believing in me. Every woman should be so blessed to have a man like you in their life. I love doing life with you. Now that this book is done, you can have your wife back! Love you pieces and pieces.

About the Author

Kim Gjerde is the adoptive mother of two amazing children and the proud step-mom to two combat Marine veterans. When she isn't teaching elementary school or driving to sports practices, you can find Kim on an airplane heading for another adventure or sitting around a campfire with her friends and family. She lives in Frederick, Maryland with her Norwegian husband Olav, their two youngest children, and their faithful beagle. *Fierce Love* is her first book.

Connect with her on social media at:
Facebook @ Kim Gjerde
Instagram @ fiercelovememoir

Or connect online at:
https://fiercelovememoir.wixsite.com/website

Thank you for reading *Fierce Love: One Woman's Remarkable Journey to Adopt her Daughter from Guatemala*. If you enjoyed my story, I would be extremely grateful if you would leave a review at Amazon and/or Goodreads.

Made in the
USA
Middletown, DE